Praise for *Chacolata*

Jerry Fabyanic's novella, *Chacolata*, takes the reader on a trip to one of his favorite spots, Chaco National Historic Park in New Mexico. Even if you are a regular visitor to this special area, you will be delightfully surprised and mystified at the turn of events as the story unfolds. Vivid descriptions of the magnificent vistas, trails, and landscape are combined with emotional thoughts and musings. You will be surprised by the appearance of two creatures that have never before been encountered. Jerry is a master storyteller. In this novella, he skillfully blends fiction and nonfiction in a very unique manner.

> – Andrea Antico, Award-Winning
> Children's Books Author

Just as Jonathan felt "the tug" pulling him to Chaco Canyon, Jerry's intricate descriptions in *Chacolata* transport the reader to a realm both physical and spiritual. This passionate tale portrays the protagonist as initially conflicted, agitated, and somewhat despondent, but by allowing the Universe to whisper hints of encouragement to him, Jonathan gains understanding and feels a nudge that drives him forward. Jerry's interconnection of nature and spirituality provides a story that will resonate with a deeper perception of life long after *Chacolata* is finished.

– Judith Janson, Retired Teacher

This story examines life. It helps you think of your own, looking for answers when you don't even know the questions. It is about emotional and spiritual growth. Are your eyes open? Jerry is a great educator. He doesn't just live life; he is always making you think about it!

– Pat Hughes Foote, Educator

Jerry Fabyanic's novella is brilliant, powerful, and so eloquently written that you won't soon forget. Although you won't want to put the book down, you'll need to stop and ponder on the spiritual search for answers to the meaning of life.

– Verena Anderson, Retired Director
of the Berlitz Language Center in Denver, Colorado

Buried under the weight of our fast-paced lives lies a yearning to know more: a yearning to uncover the mystery of forces beyond our simple lives and reveal the truth about the cycle of life, from our past to what lies ahead for us. *Chacolata* takes the reader on a journey to and through the beauty of the sacred land of Chaco Canyon. It is a beautifully told tale that heightens in the reader the desire to take their own journey of discovery.

– Mary Lou Secor, Retired Teacher, Lifelong Learner
and Seeker of Spiritual Enlightenment

Stunningly and sensually evocative in detail, Fabyanic's *Chacolata* takes readers on Jonathan's journey to find answers to questions he cannot yet vocalize. While he learns that "once something exists or happens, it endures forever," he also learns the more important lesson that "you're never alone." Strikingly surreal scenes with spirit guides will leave readers wondering about—and in awe of—the natural world surrounding them.

> – Laurel McHargue, Award-Winning Author
> of the *Waterwight* Series, Podcast Host

CHACOLATA

Also by Jerry Fabyanic

Sisyphus Wins

The Lion's Den: Book Two in the Sisyphus Series

Food for Thought: Essays on Mind and Spirit, Volume One

Food for Thought: Essays on Mind and Spirit, Volume Two

CHACOLATA

JERRY FABYANIC

Western Exposure
Georgetown, CO

Chacolata
Jerry Fabyanic
Copyright © 2024 by Jerry Fabyanic

Published by Western Exposure

Western Exposure
Georgetown, Co 80444
www.JerryFabyanic.com

ISBN (print): 978-0-9969636-6-4
ISBN (e-book): 978-0-9969636-7-1
LCCN: 2024910786

Editing by Melanie Mulhall, Dragonheart.
www.TheDragonheart.com
Cover and interior design by Nick Zelinger.
www.NZGraphics.com

First Edition
Printed in the United States of America

Dedicated to my father, Albert R. Fabyanic

Author's photographs of Chaco Culture National Historic Park sites

Front Cover: View of Pueblo Bonito from the Mesa
Part 1: Pueblo Bonito
Part 2: Chetro Ketl
Part 3: Pueblo del Arroyo
Chapter headings: Petroglyph from
the Petroglyph Trail

PART 1

CROSSING THE THRESHOLD

I LOOKED UP from the crossword I was immersed in and squinted through the windshield at the continuing drizzle. Rivulets of rain meandering their ways down the window blurred the scene. Beyond, a leaden sky and gray fog enshrouded the valley. There was no hint of the rain torrents letting up. The time on my phone said it was 1:14 PM. I tossed the newspaper with the crossword I planned to work on and pen onto the passenger seat and groped for the lever to recline my seat. Once I located it, I pushed down, eased back, and closed my eyes.

Stillness wrapped Chaco Canyon. All I could hear was rain lightly pattering on the truck roof and windows, and I focused on their mesmerizing sounds, trying to determine a pattern. Then I caught myself thinking when I should have been detaching and allowing the sounds to help calm my restless thoughts. Their magic slowly relaxed me, but the chugging of a diesel engine from an approaching vehicle soon disturbed the quiet. I cracked my eyelids to watch an old, light-tan pickup weighted by a camper shell crawl by, passing the restrooms that sat across the increasingly muddy road.

I shut my eyes and listened as the truck sounds indicated that the truck had slowed, stopped, and after a bout of grinding gears, backed up. They probably found their campsite, I thought. I listened to the truck's distinctive idling for a short time until the engine was turned off. A moment later, after hearing doors slamming, I slit my eyes again to see a man and a woman with hooded, bowed heads and hands in pockets striding briskly toward the restrooms. Again I closed my eyes and refocused my attention on the pattering drops pinging off the roof and window.

Pulling the serape I had blanketed myself in tighter, I snuggled more deeply into the seat, dry and warm despite the cool, wet conditions. The protection the truck provided was comforting. I ran a scan of my state of mind. I was beyond exhaustion, depleted mentally and spiritually. Physically, I felt listless. I followed my thoughts back ten hours to the early morning when I'd sat in my driveway debating whether to make the drive to Chaco. It would take eight hours, assuming good weather, no road detours, and no vehicle problems. Yet I knew I had to go, whatever the reason might be.

—∽—

Over the previous weeks, I had been feeling *the tug*, the sense I got from time to time that something was pulling me to Chaco. Usually, it arose when my spiritual energies were nearing depletion or when I had entered a liminal space that portended a major shift in my life's course. I had been running on fumes. Things had already been onerous due to multiple life events, but the crushing blow was the news that we—he and I—were through. The news hit like a bombshell and exacerbated my edgy state of mind. I felt betrayed and became filled with intense anger. Still, despite the depressed state that clouded my vision, I strongly felt there was something else about the tug. What that was I couldn't ascertain in my mind. All I knew was that I had to go, even if it was at an emotionally inconvenient time. A concern like the breakup of a relationship would not be allowed to stand in its way.

To say the least, I was conflicted, but there was no avoiding what had been heaped onto my plate. I had to deal with all of it, which made getting ready and loading the truck the previous afternoon—something I once relished and dived into when prepping for a trek to Chaco—burdensome, an unwanted chore far worse than the one I assiduously avoided: dusting the furniture.

As I pulled the equipment and supplies together, I'd felt I was spinning my wheels, going back over tasks I couldn't remember if I'd done. Almost always, I had. Nonetheless, I was convinced I would forget to do something like set the lamp timers or lock up before pulling out. I finally surrendered, concluding that whatever I might have missed wouldn't imperil me. The essentials were taken care of. I had topped off the gas tank and had the oil changed and the tires and brakes inspected. All was good with the truck. As for the camping gear and apparel, I would make do with whatever happened. It was neither life nor death.

Shifting my weight and dropping my head onto my right shoulder, I pictured in my mind backing out of the driveway and making my way down through the town to the interstate. The pre-dawn sky had been clear and pocked with stars, and the autumnal equinox had officially occurred a couple of hours earlier. The thought of it encouraged me to follow through with the plan I had made months earlier to spend a few days at Chaco Culture National Historic Park for some much needed spiritual practice.

Spiritually, the equinoxes and the solstices were significant markers for the ancient Chacoans, who considered the days sacred. When constructing their buildings, they had closely aligned nearly every building in accordance with the movements of the sun and moon. When the light of the sun or moon shone on those days, the light and the shadows they created marked significant moments in time and junctures or turning points in the cycle of life. The Chacoans also etched and painted glyphs throughout the valley that spoke to and about the Chacoan interpretation of the universe. For them, the valley was the center of the universe, the place where they spiritually and energetically reconnected with the Ultimate. A millennium later, it had become likewise for me. My parched soul thirsted to be quenched by the spiritual waters flowing through that dry, stark land.

Over the past couple of decades, I had made the drive multiple times, and this one promised to be just as routine as previous ones. At that early hour, few others were on the road, but thirty minutes into it, I realized my wits were not completely present. I nearly missed the exit from the interstate at Copper Mountain onto the two-lane road I would navigate through the high country. After a last second veer onto the exit ramp, I lowered the window to allow the cool pre-dawn breeze to cascade over me and inhaled deeply the sweet pine smells to stir my brain cells into action and awaken my mind. It worked, but simultaneously, it also had an intoxicating effect. The near complete darkness through which I navigated the climbing, twisting turns up to and over Fremont Pass toward Leadville became strangely mesmerizing, almost hypnotic. Though I had driven it dozens of times during the day and night, I felt as if I were coursing along a road I had never taken before. My brain told me that was not the case, but something from within suggested it was.

As I followed the Arkansas River, descending from Leadville toward Buena Vista, breaking-dawn light filtering through clouds hovering over the Mosquito Range broke the spell. Once the enchantment was broken, I regained a semblance of control and felt alert. Sights became more vivid and sounds more acute, but I also felt as if I were observing my surroundings with detachment. Curiously, I was present but simultaneously in another time and place.

I slipped an Enya CD into the player, allowing her gentle voice to enhance the symmetry of the moment. Settling into the drive, I made my way over Poncha Pass heading south and then west toward Wolf Creek Pass. After one pit stop, I climbed the pass and then cruised down to Pagosa Springs and westward to Durango. Heading south from there on US 550, I crossed the state line into New Mexico. It felt good. In another hour or so, I would turn from the paved highway onto the uneven, winding county road and then onto the unimproved, potentially rough dirt road to Chaco Canyon.

The drive southward toward Chaco Canyon, however, began inauspiciously. Dark clouds were forming to the southwest, right over where the park lay. A tad of apprehension crept in. The county gravel-and-tar road leading to the north Chaco road was in relatively good shape, but I knew the good road would soon give way to the last sixteen miles that were body-jarring under the best conditions and treacherous when saturated, taxing a vehicle and its driver.

Compounding the challenge was a wash the road traversed that could become a raging wall of water in a flash during a heavy downpour. The final potential impediment to be navigated after the wash was a stretch of ruggedly rutted clay that turned into a quagmire when waterlogged through which the hardiest of vehicles churned its way. My hope was that I'd arrive before that happened, but even if I did, I might face a lengthier stay if the skies deluged the valley for a prolonged period.

I had reserved a camp spot months earlier, so in that regard, I was okay. I knew the campground well, so when I saw on the National Parks Service website that my preferred camp spot was available, I snatched it. The campsite was a good one, directly across from the restrooms and not sandwiched between other camp spots. I was well stocked with provisions—food, water, and camping gear—so I knew I'd be good there. Short of a cataclysmic deluge, I would be safe. Still, my unease increased. Ordinarily, Chaco was dry, warm, and sunny when I visited. That's what I had anticipated and hoped for, but it was looking like that wasn't to be. Instead of Chaco being the elixir that would bring cessation to my mind's turmoil and soothe my heart, it would likely only exacerbate both. Best laid plans, I thought.

Most often, I timed my arrival for late in the afternoon, about an hour before the visitor center closed, so I could get the requisite day pass. Otherwise, I'd need to wait until 9:00 AM for the center to open. By that hour, I was invariably well into my hike, given how I loved entering the park when the ranger unlocked the gate at 7:00 so I could have it to myself, at least for a short time. Besides, in my considered opinion, anyone who didn't get up and at it at first light was a slacker.

But this time, I had planned to arrive midday to get a short hike in before dusk. I did arrive just after noon, but as I pulled into the visitor center parking lot, a gentle rain began to fall. Initially, it was soft, almost mist-like. Though disappointing, the light fog hovering over the valley gave it a mystical atmosphere. The dozen vehicles in the parking lot implied that a decent number of visitors were waiting it out, perhaps asking the rangers the same questions I would ask: How much rain is expected and how long is it supposed to last? I pulled my windbreaker over my hoodie and walked quickly to the center.

Warm and dry, the visitor center was welcoming, helping negate the gloom I was feeling. I was back in my community. Individuals dressed like me in hiking clothes leisurely sauntered around surveying scenes artistically portrayed. Others huddled around the bookshelves browsing through works on the history, art, and culture of the Chacoans and the history of the valley, all the way back to its prehistoric past. A few people fingered potential souvenirs while others with bent heads studied a large model of the valley that spread across the expanse of a long, wide table. One couple stood at the counter chatting with the ranger.

As I waited my turn, I absorbed the warmth and breathed in the energy. Even though the center was a man-made edifice full of stuff, it spoke to those who believed as I did. Chaco was not just another ancient ruin to be checked off one's bucket list after exploring it. It was wholly different, even a sacred place, one of Earth's powerful energy centers.

I stepped up to the counter. "I probably have the same question everyone else has. What's the forecast?"

"The rain is predicted to increase, but it will likely let up in a couple of hours and end by the evening," the ranger replied. He shrugged. "But then, who knows?"

I nodded in agreement. The weather cooperated most times I went there, but on a few occasions, it had been unpleasant, like the April when the rain turned to snow and I spent a very chilly, uncomfortable night shivering in my sleeping bag in the back of my old Explorer. I hadn't slept a wink that night, but the snow-covered landscape the dawn presented was beyond worth beholding, as was the drive out on the south road, which often disappeared underneath the white blanket. I smiled internally recalling that time as it flashed through my mind.

I secured my day pass and glanced at the stacks and racks of memorabilia, deciding to come back later to select something special as a memento of this visit. It was a custom I'd begun years earlier.

—∿—

Shifting in the seat and turning as much as I could to my left, I stared out the side window at the rivulets that trickled down the pane and the soggy wetness beyond. The emotional warmth I felt at my core began to dissipate. The scene was depressing. The campground was beginning to show the effects of the steady rain. Little ponds of brown water pocked the road as it grew more mucky in the tire tracks. The dry shrubs and grasses wilted under the strain of the steady rain. Tiny streams ran around the picnic tables, and the fire-pits became mushes of ash. I sighed. The world out there looked as bleak as I felt.

After what seemed an eon, I sat upright and checked my phone for the time: 1:57. Not even an hour had passed. It would be a long afternoon and evening. And night. I reached for the crossword I'd set aside, looked at it, and deciding my brain was like the firepits, too mushy to give it the concentration it required, tossed it again onto the passenger seat. Thoughts began to arise, ones that got to the deep hurt and anger I felt for my friend's betrayal, his uncaring dismissiveness, and his unappreciative attitude for the support I'd given him over the years. I felt wounded, a victim. But when that thought came to mind, I became angry with myself and jolted upright. I loathed victimhood, and I would tolerate no space in my psyche for it. Neither helpless nor anyone's hapless fool, I would not allow myself to descend into the state of self-pity.

I reached to the backseat for my cooler and the bag with snacks. Fumbling through them, I pulled out a sports drink, along with a bag of corn chips, and began to sip and munch. The scene to the south continued to grow bleaker, and the one to the west didn't look any better. Neither looked promising. Again, I considered my options. If I opted to leave, the window for doing so was closing fast. Darkness would be approaching and the road was not one I relished navigating in dim or minimal light, even in optimal conditions. The steady, soaking rain could make the clay stretch treacherous, if not impassable, and I understood full well the folly of crossing a desert wash that instantaneously could become a raging torrent. Then I would face the long drive home.

I shook my head, trying to get control of my state of mind. Yes, I felt down, but then again, I reminded myself that I was in charge of my feelings. I couldn't easily dismiss the anger and hurt, but I need not allow the circumstances to prevent me from addressing them and being open to what had been drawing me to Chaco. After a few more nibbles and sips, I felt refreshed. I decided to head back to the visitor center to break the monotony, if nothing else.

The center was busier than it had been earlier. The milling crowd probably felt as I did. Like me, in a couple of hours they would be relegated to their tents, vehicles, or campers to hunker down for the night. Until then, they were enjoying the company and welcoming warmth the building provided, perusing the selections, watching the video about the history of the canyon, and ambling through the museum and gallery to study the scenes behind glass enclosures that depicted life as it might have been for the native peoples.

The older male ranger who had staffed the desk earlier was replaced by a young woman with long, black, braided hair. Her engaging presence struck me, so after asking for updates and seeing no one waiting behind me, I continued our conversation. She told me that she was of Native descent, born and raised nearby. From the time she was little, her parents had brought her to Chaco. They impressed on her an awareness of and appreciation for its power and importance as a central place in the universe.

When she was twelve years old, she underwent a coming-of-age initiation ritual. She was not permitted to talk about the precise ritualistic practices, but since then, she'd spent many days alone hiking, exploring, and performing rituals in the far stretches of Chaco. As she enthralled me with her personal tale, I noticed my energy being restored. When I walked away, I felt reinvigorated, but then quickly felt shame on its heels. How foolish I was to consider leaving because of a little rain. I decided to join the others and began browsing through a pile of brightly colored wool blankets, all with intricate angular patterns. Delighted to find one that struck me as especially appealing, I purchased it.

By the time I stepped outside, the rain had lightened to a mist, and I found that it no longer dampened my spirit. Instead, it felt refreshing, and I became excited anew about the prospect of getting lost in Chaco in time and place. It wasn't yet 3:00, which meant there were still a few hours of daylight remaining, so I decided to do a slow drive around the park's eight-mile loop. As I approached Pueblo Bonito, the most famous site along the course, I was pleasantly surprised. Usually, it was bustling with people, but this time, there were only a few vehicles in the lot. I decided that this would be a perfect opportunity to reexplore it.

I pulled my rain jacket over my hoodie and set forth up the pathway. Ahead on the path that connected Pueblo Bonito with Chetro Ketl, another restored site, I spotted a small group huddled under an array of brightly colored umbrellas. One person was gesticulating, pointing upward toward the petroglyphs painted on the mesa wall. I figured it was the group in the REI van exiting the parking lot when I had pulled in. Ahead and to my left, Pueblo Bonito seemed empty of human traffic. Perfect, I thought.

I walked slowly up the trail, taking my time not only to study the site but also to inhale the moisture-heavy atmosphere. It permeated my soul as it did the air around me. I smiled as I thought that in my current mental and spiritual state, I would be better served standing naked in a hellacious downpour to wash away the negative grime. Slowly, I reminded myself: Healing begins with small steps.

As I trod the path, I periodically reached out to touch a stone and paused to study the structure. As always, I imagined the daily activities of the ancients, their rituals, and their centuries-long construction, generation after generation. Not completely tearing down and replacing what their ancestors had built but carrying on the traditions, adding to and building upon that which preceded them. Timeless life in rhythm and harmony with their world and their universe, an integral part of and not separate from them—all done without a written language or apparent mathematical wizardry. Instead, they employed oral history and education handed down from one short-lived generation to the next that in turn repeated the ritual. Life without end. One continuous loop.

Circling up to the high point of Pueblo Bonito, I lifted my head and faced the now softening gray sky and allowed the soft mist to bathe my face. I extended my arms upward and outward and inhaled deeply. As I exhaled, I looked down to a lower tier and caught site of a woman casually strolling across the courtyard. She was wearing a cowboy hat adorned with feathers that were resisting the weight of the rain, a Western-style jacket, and a long denim skirt. The jacket and skirt were embroidered with some indistinguishable artwork. It was clear that I wasn't the sole sojourner appreciating the solitude of Pueblo Bonito, but it was okay. Pueblo Bonito was not mine to possess, and it pleased me that another person seemed to be finding it captivating.

With no chance of my boots drying out overnight, I tried to be careful not to slosh through the puddles like I loved doing when a boy, although it was tempting. Even as an old man, I liked to frolic, so I skirted and leapt as best I could over puddles as I made my way through the complex. At times I needed to duck low and pull my arms tightly to my sides to squeeze through portals. Periodically, I paused to observe and feel the sandstone. After crawling through one portal into an enclosed room with a soft sand floor, I glanced up and noticed the woman I saw a few minutes earlier in the next room. She was sitting in a meditative, half lotus position. Immediately, she turned and smiled.

"I thought I heard you step in," she said pleasantly.

I was taken aback. Between not talking and the soft, sandy flooring, I was confident I'd made no or little sound.

"I'm sorry to have disturbed you," I replied.

The woman stood and dusted the sand from her skirt. As she did, I took in the exquisite embroidery of various birds including an owl, myna, and eagle on her skirt.

"You didn't," she said pointing to the aperture. "Climb in. I think you'd like to see this."

I climbed through the portal and stooped to peek through the open space that served as a window. "Wow! That's incredible. Even through the mist, the light seems to dance."

"Have you been in here before?" she asked after I straightened up.

"I come to Chaco often, but I haven't been through this site in a long time. I tend to pass by it since there usually are lots of people meandering around and chattering. And you?"

"I come here often. I love sitting perched on a wall or some other spot like an outcropping. But it's been some time for me too. Life always seems to get in the way of my coming back."

"Where are you from?"

"My nesting place is in Tucson, but I like to winter in Mexico. In the spring, I head north. I like to travel. Fly wherever my wings will take me. I made plans to get here for the equinox. I was fortunate to get here a few days ago."

"So you were here this morning. Was it clear at sunrise?"

"It was dazzling. It had rained to the east, but it stayed dry here. There were clouds hovering, but there weren't any on the horizon. When the sun rose, it beamed through this window. It was brilliant. I was able to sit on the ledge and take it in."

I stooped again to peer through the opening and regretted the fact that I'd missed it. "A day late," I muttered in a deflated voice as I shook my head.

The woman continued. "Legend has it that it rarely rains here on the autumnal equinox, which means the dawn never disappoints. The sun pours shafts of light through the east facing windows in all the buildings."

We talked about the architecture, the layout of the structures, and how the structures are all aligned with the paths of the sun at the solstices and equinoxes and the moon in its phases. I felt exhilarated. I had met a kindred soul who viewed the world and universe as I did and spoke that language.

When the conversation wound down, I extended my hand and introduced myself formally. "Jonathan," I said.

"Ann," she replied as she shook my hand. She stooped to climb out through the portal and turned her head toward me. "The answer to your question is in here," she said before climbing through.

I was flummoxed, slack-jawed, convinced that I presented myself in a positive, upbeat manner and was completely present in the moment. But Ann seemed to read my energy. It took me aback. We'd only been together for a few minutes, yet she'd seen deeply within me and sensed something important. She knew I was not all right. Inside, I was a mess. Something was amiss, and that something had to be reckoned with.

I scrunched down, sat back on my haunches in front of the aperture, and stared at the misty rain. Stretching my arms wide, I cupped my hands and touched my thumbs to my middle fingers while closing my eyes and inhaling deeply. I inflated my lungs fully, held the breath, and expelled it in a full gust, repeating the practice twice. After the third exhalation, I felt a flood of emotion wash over me. All that I held inside burst forth and spewed like a geyser. I shuddered and gasped before leaping to my feet and bellowing plaintively to the Universe.

"I don't know where to begin. I'm filled with anger. I'm frustrated and tired. Exhausted mentally, physically, and spiritually." I breathed deeply, exhaled forcefully twice more, then continued. "I know my problems don't compare with the suffering millions and even billions are experiencing, but right now, they're overwhelming."

Holding my posture rigid, I stood still. The silence was deafening. No one answered. Not even an echo. All I could hear was my heavy breathing. Momentarily though, I sensed a wave of cool energy wash over me, dousing the heated passion. I pictured the firepit, only this time, I saw it not laden with soggy ash but having been rinsed clean, the mucky mess flushed from it out onto the ground to be absorbed by the earth. I felt my heartbeat slowing and my breath softening. Then a thought entered my mind as if an inner voice were speaking to me. *It's just stuff.*

Simple as all that. It was just stuff, none of it critical or essential. In my mind, I pictured stepping away and observing myself. I focused on my woundedness and my sense of victimhood, which caused me such self-loathing, and I was repulsed by it. In the place of a strong and determined character, I saw a weak, pathetic figure. I pictured the dragon Joseph Campbell described as a powerful motif in Western mythologies. The ego. I had to confront and slay it.

I stepped back into ordinary consciousness for a moment. "Big deal," I said softly and soothingly. "So your feelings were hurt. And you might be out of the money you fronted him to furnish his apartment, but so what?"

A sense of calmness took hold. I did a body scan, beginning with wiggling my toes and working my way up to and through my crown. Then I stepped outside of my body again and took a hard look. "Yep, still in one piece. All's intact. Nothing's changed," I whispered. After a pause, I added, "Except everything."

Folding my hands in prayer fashion, I breathed deeply and rhythmically, exhaling completely, this time without intentional force. Detachment. Stillness. No thought. Just being.

—m—

The drive back from Pueblo Bonito along the eight-mile-loop road allowed the heater to dispel the remaining chill. It was near dusk, albeit dusk having come early due to the lingering heavy clouds and mist. There would be no firing up the camp stove to boil water for soup or tea this evening. Back at my campsite, the inside of the cab once again felt cozy. It and I were dry. I felt a good tiredness, like every muscle relaxing after a strenuous workout.

After flipping on my flashlight and peering into my cooler, I pulled out a bagel with cream cheese and the bag of corn chips. I took small bites, chewing slowly and deliberately, and nibbled on the crisp chips, chasing them with a sports drink. It was a cold but filling and fulfilling supper. After I finished my repast, I wrapped the woven woolen blanket I had purchased earlier around me. As the birds embroidered on Ann's skirt brought her skirt to life, so too did the traditional Native American patterns bring it to life. The geometric patterns were a blend of deep forest green and crimson red, accentuated by bone-white striping extending from a light-brown center square. I rubbed my hand over the wool, absorbed its warmth, and checked the label, which said it was made in El Paso.

Sighing in contentment, I fumbled through the items on the passenger seat in search of the crossword I set aside earlier and got to work on it. Shortly after, it seemed, I looked up to see that night had completely fallen in the time I was absorbed in the puzzle. I smiled in satisfaction. It was almost complete with only a few letters and words scratched over. My ongoing goal was to nail it with none. Another time.

I set the newspaper on the passenger seat, flipped off the flashlight, and stared out at the darkness. Stillness reigned. The only indication of neighbors was the soft lighting from their campers seeping into the darkness. It's good, I thought. Very good.

Thoughts of meeting Ann, my chat with her, and the events of the afternoon ruminated through my mind when I closed my eyes. Suddenly, the stillness felt accentuated. It dawned on me that it was absolutely quiet. I cracked the truck door open to confirm that the rain had stopped. It had.

The ground was sodden when I stepped out onto it, but the air was sweet. I tilted my head back and stared at the ebony overhead blanket and surmised that the rain had probably stopped for good, debating whether to flip back the truck bed's hard cover shell and sleep, as per my practice, under the open sky or to burrow underneath it. Even if the storm had moved on, it was not likely there would be any stars appearing, but there still remained the potential for a light rain shower. I decided not to risk it. Even if it didn't rain again, in all probability, fog would form and soak my bag, making sleeping an unpleasant experience. I smiled thinking of that time when I froze my butt off here and shivered thinking of it.

"Once was enough," I murmured, chuckling.

I flipped the flashlight back on, gathered the items from the cab I would need for the night, and hauled them to the back of the truck. After dropping the tailgate and tossing my equipment in, I crawled under the shell. It was a tight squeeze with only about twelve inches clearance, so I had to wiggle to get under it. I was pleased to see that despite the steady rain, the truck bed's carpeting and contents had remained relatively dry. My bag was slightly damp, but not uncomfortably so. After pulling off my boots, I squirmed to arrange the sleeping pad, plumped my pillow, and pulled my sleeping bag over me. Then I flipped off the flashlight and lay back, staring at the dark bed cover. It was pitch-black and so quiet that the stillness echoed. I felt snug, dry, and warm. Nice, I thought. So peaceful. What a day. Much gratitude.

—◊—

I peered out through the opened tailgate to complete darkness at 5:00 AM. Quiet and stillness continued to reign, and I decided to wait thirty minutes before venturing forth. When I did, I found myself wrapped in an embracing fog that had settled over the Chacoan valley. I shined my flashlight in the direction of the restrooms and was bedazzled as I walked toward them by the minuscule rivulets of moisture flowing through the beam, like sprinkles of microscopic water particles being gently carried by an imperceptible breeze.

After taking care of my morning ablutions and changing into fresh clothing suitable for the day ahead, I stepped from the restroom to see hints of daylight appearing on the eastern horizon. Though I moved stealthily to avoid disturbing the other campers, I saw that several had also begun stirring. I flipped back the truck bed's shell as quietly as I could, pulled out my camp stove and plastic bins filled with gear, and set them on the picnic table.

With the stove lit and water boiling to brew green tea, I enjoyed another bagel smothered with cream cheese and found some fruit I'd brought with me. As I chewed and sipped my tea, I stared up into the dawning light. I miss this, I thought. Not only did I miss camping but also making pilgrimages to Chaco. They were treasures from my past I had put away with the promise I would revisit them at some future time, a time that rarely came anymore. But now the time had come, and with it the realization of what I had lost—or better put, given up. I surveyed the scene unfolding around me, again noted that I was with my tribe, and vowed not to lose moments like these and be separated from my tribal members again, frittering away the most valuable treasure one has: the now.

By the time I finished my bagel, tea, and fruit, the campground seemed to have completely stirred from its slumber. Activity spread throughout, not with speech but with the clatter of camp stoves and cookware. It was a twenty-first century version of Chacoan life, and there was serenity to it. Here, bustle was not a characteristic of my waking tribe. I exchanged waves with a man walking his dog through the brush behind my camp spot.

I brewed a second cup of tea to sip while I drove through the park, cleaned and packed my equipment, and loaded it back into the truck bed. Ten minutes later, I maneuvered out of my campsite and slowly navigated the mucky road, taking care to ease my tires through puddles I couldn't avoid. Several campers waved as I crawled by, and I returned their greetings. Those morning greetings were to me akin to tribal acknowledgments. As I approached the park entrance, a ranger who had apparently just unlocked the gate was climbing back into her pickup. Right on time, I thought. I waved and she waved back.

It was the first full day following the autumnal equinox. The morning fog was becoming less dense but still blanketed the valley. Faint sunrays filtered through the silver clouds. The once brown vegetation that had strained under the weight of the raindrops was emanating life and renewed vigor. Seemingly, it was making a statement about there still being life to live, albeit short, before the inevitable frost. I slowed as I passed Pueblo Bonito and thought again of Ann and her declaration. *The answer to your question is in here.*

Shortly ahead, I bore right onto the spur that led to Kin Kletso, where the trail to Pueblo Alto lay and the one out to Peñasco Blanco began. Ordinarily, hiking to both would be on my to-do list, but with the rains, the trail out and up to Peñasco Blanco wouldn't be feasible given it was largely sand with clay stretches and crossed a creek, which would likely be swollen and moving with a steady current. But I knew the mesa trail above would be very doable, at least for the first part, since it traversed a rock surface, though the trail up to Pueblo Alto had a couple of stretches of clay. I laced up my boots, double-checked my pack to be sure I had all I would need, and slipped my phone into my cargo shorts pocket. Then I tugged on and tightened the straps of my daypack and set off for Kin Kletso.

CALL FROM THE WILD

THE CREVICE I crawled through had been created millions of years ago, and I paused as I took in the breathtaking scene. The air smelled sweet with sage and was cool and fresh. I was taking a slow inhalation when a howl caught my attention, and I looked back over my shoulder in the direction of Peñasco Blanco. When I heard the second howl, there was no doubt: The sound was real and coming from a coyote, its high-pitched howl echoing off the rocky mesa floor and surroundings. In all the years I'd come to Chaco, I'd never heard one. In fact, the one time I ever heard real-life coyotes had been twelve years earlier when I'd put my chocolate lab, Augie, to sleep. Twelve years to the day. That was an uncanny coincidence.

Too emotional to be functional, the day following his death, I decided to hike up to the tarn that Augie and I regularly climbed to. As with this time, I'd made the climb at first light and was hiking alone. After the initial half mile of my ascent, I heard coyotes yipping. At first, their howls unnerved me, but after a while they seemed less threatening. In fact, their yips increasingly felt strangely inviting and comforting. They seemed to be calls from the wild letting me know Augie was romping free with them. And here again was at least one. I pushed on.

Thoughts jumbled my mind as I stepped across the rocks, breaking from them only to note the cairns that marked the trail. The chance encounter with Ann and the sequence of events leading to that moment remained vivid. It had to be synchronicity, for if I had tarried five or ten minutes, it might not have happened. Some force had to have moved me to that place at that precise time. My job was not to overthink it but to remain present and trust the Universe—wherever it was leading me.

Lost in my thoughts, I was surprised when I spotted the sign for the Pueblo Bonito Overlook just ahead of me. I hadn't realized I had come that far. I paused to scan the horizon. A thin cloud cover blanketed the expanse of the valley with the morning sun faintly hovering behind it. The landscape emanated a golden hue. I took a deep breath. The air was moist and clean. It then dawned on me that I no longer heard the coyote. Only quiet.

I veered off the main trail and picked my way toward the overlook. It would be great, I thought, to get a picture of Pueblo Bonito from above. I hoped there wouldn't be other visitors and soon discovered I was in luck. The site was vacant. There were no cars in the parking lot, although several were approaching. I needed to hurry. Ann again came to mind, and I realized as I snapped the picture that I'd forever associate Pueblo Bonito with her.

I turned and retraced my steps to the main trail and quickly spotted the spur that led up to Pueblo Alto. I climbed up the rock steps that led to the path, and at the top, I surveyed the vista due north to where the Chacoan ancients' most sacred site sat.

To the uncurious, the Chacoan mesa might look unremarkable, ordinary. The terrain—flat light-brown sandstone rock broken by stretches of scrub brush—is uninterrupted openness. No trees or willowy, lush bushes. But for the attentive, the Chacoan mesa is rife with mystery. One could easily imagine it not looking much, if any, different to the ancients. You could presume that to them, it wasn't dull, but extraordinary and even sacred. For several centuries, they traversed it in pilgrimage to their most sacred site, Pueblo Alto. There they smashed intricately molded and painted pottery, sacrificing and offering them in homage to their ancestral spirits.

As I got closer to the site, I felt a sense of anticipation arising within me. I resisted focusing on it and kept an attentive eye on the path. Though mostly defined and visible, the path could instantly disappear as it coursed its way over sandstone outcroppings and through the scrub brush. Abruptly, I pulled up and scanned left to right. Something told me I wasn't alone, that another was also trekking the mesa. Ahead near cairns marking the trail, I caught a glimpse of movement darting through the brush and focused my gaze in that direction, to the northwest toward New Alto, a partially restored sister site to Pueblo Alto. I couldn't see anything unusual and concluded it might have been a rabbit or some other small critter. That would explain the presence of coyotes. Seeing and hearing nothing disturbing, I continued north.

A short distance ahead, there was a stretch of mucky clay, and I could see the patch stretched for a distance. I'd have to step cautiously, given how one slip would make for an unpleasant experience. I silently reprimanded myself for not bringing my hiking sticks.

Not seeing an alternative after surveying both sides, I stepped gingerly into the mire, keeping to the right because it seemed less oozy there. I trod slowly and deliberately, grabbing hold of shrub branches and carefully placing each footstep to lessen the potential of slipping. A few steps into the muck, indentations in it that looked like paw prints caught my eye, and crouching, I squinted for a closer view. They were fresh. When I stood back up and scanned the area, I saw nothing irregular. I continued on, and after traversing the muck without incident, I scraped what I could of the heavy residue from my boots against a rock.

A short distance farther, a weathered sign with two arrows stood at the trail junction. One arrow pointed left toward New Alto and the other to Pueblo Alto. As

I was about to veer off to the right and pick my way up to the Pueblo Alto, I caught sight of a man hiking across the path that connected New Alto with Pueblo Alto. He was small in structure and had a rucksack strapped to his back. Directly ahead, he stopped and turned to the north. Wanting to be respectful by giving him space, I simply noted his presence and picked my way up the hillside to the Pueblo Alto site.

For the first-time visitor, Pueblo Alto might be indistinguishable from the rest of the terrain. Consequently, it lacks the drawing power the restored sites hold. But that wasn't the case with me from the start. Even after numerous treks to the site, I find myself filled with awe anew each time I visit it. And that day was no exception. Still, something felt off, odd even, though nothing looked unusual. And although the complexity of the structure remained intact, it seemed different, as if it had taken on and was radiating a more vibrant energy.

I stood at the perimeter and scanned the site, again wondering if the ancients had planned the layout or if they constructed it haphazardly. The maze of square rooms and round kivas still boggled my mind. Did the shapes of the rooms indicate different purposes? The evidence and tradition suggested the circular rooms—kivas—were for ceremonial rites. But what about the square and rectangular ones? Were they all for rituals or perhaps were some used for instruction like modern-day classrooms? I wondered too about the powers they might have had. Did they hold the power of allowing the ancients to see through the portal of time and space in ways our Western minds find unfathomable? Did the Chacoans, as has been suggested, become so powerful that they could control the powers of nature? If so, they would have been able to defy the laws of physics, but then, so would the miracles Jesus is purported to have performed.

As I surveyed the landscape, I paid close attention to the details of the meticulously cut and layered sandstone walls and focused on the detritus of pottery shards intermixed with the high desert flora, each gradually returning from whence it came: Mother Earth. I stretched my arms wide and then folded them into an embrace. Then I noticed something I didn't recall seeing in the center of a kiva on prior visits: a round, three-inch-thick sandstone slab that was about eighteen inches in diameter. Its perimeter was beveled, and its center was splotched white. For it to have remained in such a place and in such remarkable condition for a millennium seemed highly unlikely. More likely, I concluded, it was placed there by more recent visitors, perhaps for performing rituals that might or might not be in the tradition of the ancients.

After dropping down into that kiva, I leaned my daypack against the kiva's stone wall and stepped up onto the rock. I faced east, stretched my arms skyward, and began my seven-direction ritual. I rotated clockwise, stopping at each cardinal direction to reflect on what they symbolized: east, new days and beginnings; south, bounteous life; west, change and transition; and north, wisdom, love, and eternity. As I faced each direction, I correlated it to the three lower chakras and to the fourth, heart chakra, offering gratitude and asking for continual guidance. Focusing on the fifth chakra, I stooped and touched the earth. For the sixth, I reached skyward to the firmament, and for the seventh, I extended my arms wide and slowly pivoted, taking in all I could hold through each of my senses as I acknowledged the circle of life.

When I completed the ritual, I closed my eyes and stood comfortably erect with arms drooped to my sides and my chin resting softly near my right shoulder. I could feel the fatigue and anxiety easing and draining. I felt physically exhausted, like after a fever that has broken, but mentally and spiritually serene. I remained like that for several minutes, dismissing wayward thoughts that randomly popped into consciousness, continually bringing my mind to the present and focusing my attention solely on what I could absorb through my senses. Then I slowly twisted my head from side to side to relieve the tension in my neck and shoulders and finally opened my eyes. Was I having another vision? On the kiva wall directly ahead sat the man I espied earlier.

The man's thick, dark hair was cropped unevenly and hung nearly to his shoulders. A wide leather headband embossed with a mix of geometrical patterns punctuated by sketches of animals and other images of nature covered his forehead. Deep lines creasing his cheeks pointed upward to dark-chocolate eyes. His nose was flat and wide and his chin curved gracefully. His lips were full; his skin leathered and copper in tone. His shirt and leggings were a patchwork of woven fiber and leather punctuated by a fiber sash tied at his waist. A pelt rested on his shoulders, its forelegs draping over and across his breast with its hindlegs dangling near his waist. A rucksack sat by his side.

"I did not want to disturb your ceremony," he said. His voice had a soft resonance to it, neither high-pitched nor deep, and his speech was halting.

"You didn't," I replied. "When I first saw you there, I thought I was having a vision, but as I focused, I realized you were real."

"Yes, I am. I am real, but only for those whose eyes are open."

"I saw you a short while ago walking toward here from that other site."

"Yes, I know. I saw you too. I watched you hiking along the trail." The man lifted one of the pelt forelegs and pointed it at me, twirling it in a circular motion. "That's an interesting ceremony you performed there. I've not seen anything like it."

"It's something I adapted from a spiritual guru I once followed."

"Guru. I am not familiar with that word."

"A guru is a spiritual leader and teacher who has an understanding of the deeper nature of things."

"Do all gurus know of such things?"

"No. Some are frauds. In fact, most are in my opinion."

"I see." He motioned to my daypack. "Please sit. You must be tired after the climb up from the canyon."

"I am. I'm pretty exhausted, but not because of that." I sat and pulled two granola bars from my pack. "Can I offer you one?"

"No, thank you. I eat only natural food."

"These are natural. Organic."

"I mean foods directly from the land. I have never been able to digest anything man-made."

"I understand that," I said conversationally.

"You say you thought you were having another vision. Have you had a vision here before?"

"Many years ago, I saw my mother and brother appear out of a swirling vortex while doing the same ceremony."

"Vortex. Another word I do not know."

"It's like a spinning mass of air or energy."

"Like a windstorm?"

"Yes. That's a good analogy." Seeing confusion on the man's face, I clarified. "A good comparison."

"Have you had others?"

"Maybe. Yesterday in the Pueblo Bonito site. I'm beginning to wonder if the person I talked to was real."

"Ann?"

I looked surprised. "You know her?"

"I know her well. She is my sister."

"Wow. I would not have made that connection. You don't resemble each other at all."

"That is because we are from different tribes. She flies; I run. But we are all one in the Great Spirit."

"Huh. Interesting." I tore open a package, took a bite, and chewed slowly, trying to digest what the man said. He sat in silence. Redirecting the conversation, I asked, "Do you live nearby?"

"Yes. Very nearby."

"Inside the park boundaries?"

"We do not know boundaries. We share the land with all our cousins. We have lived here forever."

"Forever is a long time."

"It is, and then it is not." He lifted the foreleg again and pointed it at me. "I have seen you here before."

I was startled. "You have?"

"Many times. Usually you hike up here, and then after you climb back down from the mesa, you hike to the Great House your people call Peñasco Blanco. After you climb up to it, you always eat a meal. My brothers go in after you leave to see if you dropped anything worth eating, like a piece of meat. But you never do."

His words startled me. I never considered that I might be surreptitiously watched. "I take care to leave no trace other than my footprints. I detest people who disrespect nature by carelessly not carrying out what they carry in."

The man nodded. "I watched you from the high ground as you looked down on the Great House, Pueblo Bonito."

I was more confused. Even though I understood that there were some who hiked through the park for long stretches, I could swear I was alone as I looked down at Pueblo Bonito. Hikers are supposed to register at the visitor center, but seemingly, this man was not one to go by the rules. I thought of the overlook from which the man said he saw me.

"That rock overhang is high above and east of the overlook," I said. "But I saw you approaching here from the west. You made good time to get from there to New Alto and then to here."

"I travel quickly and lightly."

I sat quietly reflecting as I munched on my granola bar. I reached into my daypack and pulled out the orange wedges I stowed in a plastic container. "Would you like some of my orange?" I asked. "It's definitely natural food."

"I do not eat fruit. Just meat and wild grain." Shifting the conversation again, the man asked, "Did you hear singing when you got up onto the mesa?"

"The coyote? I did. I never would've thought to call coyote yips and howls singing, but now that you call it that, I like it. It was fascinating and surprising. I had never heard coyotes here before."

"That is because you weren't listening. Today it was sweet music to welcome you. I am glad your ears were open this time."

"Some people become fearful when they hear them. Strangely, I don't. In fact, I find their calls comforting."

"That is good. Have you always found them comforting?"

"I used to think I would be afraid if they were nearby, but not anymore. I heard them once when I was hiking alone in the mountains. It was an enclosed area, a high valley. At first, they unnerved me, but soon I didn't feel afraid."

"Why do you think you do not feel fear now?"

"I'm not sure. Maybe it's because as I grow older, I feel more at home, safer in nature than I do in towns and cities."

The man nodded in understanding. "Now your ears are open. You listen."

"I do. And breathe and see. At least, I try to. I now take time to study and appreciate so much I used to glance past or over."

"That is good. That is why you heard the singing. It was calling you."

"Calling me?"

"Yes, for you to come home."

"Home? I don't understand."

"This land has much power. It called you from far away. It is the reason you were drawn here. It is important that you return and walk as you do in a sacred manner. It is important that you talk as you did with Ann. She is very wise. Remember what she said. The answer to your question."

I was dumbfounded. I was convinced Ann and I had been alone. My jaw dropped.

"How do you know we talked? What we said?"

"I watched you the whole time you were there. You did not see me because your eyes were still closed. When Ann left, I waited outside and listened." He paused and grimaced. "I heard much pain."

"But there was no one else around there," I insisted. "Just Ann and me."

The man's eyes softened, and a hint of a smile appeared. He uncrossed his legs, stood, and walked over to me. I stood and the man placed a paw from the pelt on my shoulder.

"You do not remember," the man said, "but you have been coming here for many, many moons—long before the times you do remember. Your memory has been clouded, fogged over, much like how this land was last night. Living in what you call civilization does that."

I shook my head, trying to unpack the enormity of what the man said. Reincarnation? Previous lives? I accepted that it could very well be true. Buddhists and others certainly believed it. And like the Resurrection, there was as much evidence to support it as there was to refute it: none.

"You have much to learn," the man said as he walked to the center of the kiva. He pointed to the ceremonial stone. "Come. Stand here."

I did as instructed and stepped onto the stone. As the man directed, I faced the east, cupped my hands, and stretched my arms upward. With my eyes closed, I lifted my face to the sun, now brightly shining, and felt its warmth wash over me and soak into my soul. I heard the man stirring behind me and then nothing other than the breeze. Until the howl. I quickly turned to see one coyote atop a knoll a short distance off. We stared at one another for a moment before he turned and bolted off in the direction of New Alto.

—ɯ—

The evening was a complete contrast to the previous one. The sky was cloudless with a sprinkling of stars making their appearances while other stars more distant waited until the campfires were doused and artificial lights switched off to make their entrances. Campers went about their business with minimal noise. Distinct sounds, voices, vehicles, and campground clatter came and went. Pleasantly, they did not form a collective hum, din, or buzz like in a city. I debated whether to build a fire, but the temperature was comfortably warm, largely due to the heat emanating from the rock cliffs of the mesa. That suggested a campfire was unnecessary to cut the chill so often felt in the open spaces when evening descended. But then again, a campfire would add to the mood. I went about building one.

I settled back in my camp chair and sipped water as I watched the last glimmer of daylight fade, noting that the bustling was subsiding but also being aware that certain sounds were becoming more acute. Campers were settling in or turning in for the evening. I gulped the clean air, enriched with sage, pinon, and other smells of the desert. The scents helped reenergize my spirit, and I felt at home despite not being a desert nomad.

Scenes from the past twenty-four hours, particularly my excursion to Pueblo Alto, flooded my mind. I worked on trying to make sense of it. I was convinced that what I'd experienced wasn't a vision. It was real, substantial. I also believed the being I had conversed with was a person. Our exchange made sense, even if some of what he shared was obscure and puzzling. But how could I explain the apparent connection between him and the coyote? Were they one and the same or were they different beings? Did he have a name? We didn't introduce ourselves like Ann and I did. But then, it didn't seem appropriate or necessary. I dubbed him Coyote Man.

"May I join you?"

I recognized the voice as soon as I heard it and turned to see Ann. She was carrying a collapsible camp chair and water bottle.

I smiled invitingly. "Of course."

"Beautiful evening," Ann said as she unfolded her chair. She placed it at an angle from mine so she too could watch the fading light disappear over the western horizon.

"It is," I replied. "I've been coming here for years and have had some incredibly amazing experiences, but nothing to this degree."

"It is breathtaking."

We both sat quietly, taking in the warmth of the evening. After a few minutes, she turned toward me and caught my eye. Her look was penetrating. "Did you get the answer to your question?"

I instantly felt my throat constricting. The heated exchange my friend and I had a few days earlier rushed back into mind. My eyes glistened and I bit my lower lip. My voice dropped to a whisper. "I did."

Ann's inviting, compassionate expression helped calm the tension that had arisen. I cleared my throat.

"After my partner, Daniel, and I separated, I became close to a charming, caring, artistic, brilliant man. We quickly bonded, but I soon saw that he struggled with multiple emotional issues. A couple of them were innate, but the rest were inflicted by others. In time, our relationship evolved into a caretaking one—with me usually taking care of him. Even though it increasingly became a one-way street, I accepted it. I couldn't abandon or reject him like others had. He'd been deeply wounded and scarred in ways only gay men can understand.

"I'll skip the details, but out of the blue, he called to say that he was altering something we had agreed to that I valued highly. He was putting another in my place. For me, it was a bridge too far. I snapped and gave him more than a piece of my mind, reminding him that my care and support of him over the years was the reason he was able to achieve what he has."

I shook my head. "I've been sort of in a daze about it, but now, although it still hurts, I'm sensing it wasn't a catastrophe."

Ann nodded and looked back to the fading light. "It's like that with most things. People get themselves tied up into knots over stuff that seems critically important, but once they're through it, they wonder why they became so agitated in the first place."

I considered Ann's observation before replying and furled my brow. "It seems, in a way, like how we're always racing, in a hurry to get somewhere. Whether we arrive on time or five or ten minutes late usually doesn't matter. Sometimes it does, of course, such as for a life-and-death emergency or a flight departure. But we tend to mix the important and trivial all into one mindset." I paused and then went on. "It seems that when *all* of life is a crisis or emergency, there's no such thing as one."

"Well said, and it's compounded and even exacerbated by the demands and pace of modern life. There isn't any down time for most. It's scurry and bustle within a whirlpool of racket. It's why many are freaked out by quiet. They simply can't handle it."

"Or solitude. I enjoy being around people and engaging in meaningful and even robust conversation, but if it becomes belabored, I find myself moving toward the door or thinking of a way to change the subject." Neither of us spoke, but after a bit, I glanced over at Ann and smiled. "This is the kind of conversation I could engage in for hours."

Ann smiled. "So you had an interesting hike up to Pueblo Alto," she said more matter-of-factly than inquisitively.

I cocked my head and then chuckled. "I was about to ask you how you would know that, but now I suspect I might know."

A coy smile appeared on her face. She tightened her brow a bit, pursed her lips, and reached into her skirt pocket. "I brought some trail mix to nibble on. Can I share it with you?"

"Thank you. I'd love some." I stretched out my hand and she sprinkled some into my palm."

"I'm not one to eat large meals. I prefer nibbling, just consuming what I need and no more," she admitted.

"Like a bird, eh?"

She smiled. "You might say that." Ann shook a small pile into her hand and nibbled. After a swig of water, she spoke again in a more serious tone. "I'm sensing that there is something else, something deeper troubling you."

I turned to stare into her eyes. Obscure thoughts ran through my head, none of which made sense. I squinted and spoke evasively. "Not that I can think of right now. Of course, I always have questions out of curiosity." I paused and sipped some water. "But then, there are times when stuff troubles me, situations or puzzling utterances that crop up out of nowhere that I cannot seem to make sense of. It's then, like now, that I find myself coming here, my most sacred place, with the hope that I can find answers to questions I don't know. But this time was different. It was as if I was being pulled here, and I'm still unsure why. If that makes sense."

"It does. I have found that people tend to block or put out of mind vexing questions if they aren't able to come up with clear-cut answers immediately. They try to suppress the anxiety they feel, but the anxiety doesn't go away. It simply gets buried or set aside only to resurface in other ways."

I nodded and broke the eye-to-eye connection, turning my gaze back to the sky. "It sounds as if you have studied Jung's notion about a person's shadow."

"I've learned much over time."

I looked at her sideways and raised an eyebrow. "Years? Maybe centuries or eons?"

Ann looked evasive. She poured herself another handful of trail mix and chewed slowly. "You're on your path, and though you apparently have learned much about life, you have much more to learn if you are to advance. Keep in mind that what seems obvious to the human mind might not be true. Humans have a tendency to consider what they literally see as reality. Solid. Definite. And that's reasonable. Some, however, sense or believe there is or has to be more behind the visible and tangible, so they search. But many of them soon find the search daunting and exhausting, so they give up and subscribe to the easiest and most convenient explanation presented, which is usually what they were taught in childhood."

"Religion?"

"I don't judge people for their choices on that, but it is true that some, like you, find religious explanations unfulfilling and too simplistic. Still, all roads lead to the Ultimate. Some are full of ruts, and pitfalls make the journeyer give up or go astray."

Ann and I sat quietly as I pondered her insights. Night had completely fallen. A comforting soft, warm breeze enveloped me. I tilted my head back and gazed at the infinite number of stars that populated the sky.

"The only downside of being here is the light pollution from the lamps," I said. "Usually, I'm asleep by the time they're all shut off, but rising before dawn gives me time to meditate on the infinite in absolute stillness."

Ann said nothing, as if waiting for me to speak. When I didn't, she spoke. "As I said before, I sense there is something troubling you, something you put on the back burner, not out of frustration but because you figured the answer would come when it needed to."

I lowered my head and turned to look at Ann. "It seems the first thing I need to do is figure out the question."

"Not necessarily. Sometimes people spin their wheels trying to identify what's troubling them and reduce it to a succinct issue rather than simply acknowledging their unease and allowing that to serve as their question. If they would detach and allow the Universe to provide answers in its own way and time, they would find that the answer provides the question."

She stood and folded her chair. "That time has arrived for you, Jonathan. Neither the question nor the answer is here. They're in another place far from here, a place you know quite well. It's there you will find the one you need to talk to."

PART 2

THE GARDEN

THE HOUSE STOOD much as it had when I left it nearly a half century before. Built a few months prior to the bombing of Pearl Harbor, it seemed timeless, as if it were meant to stand much like the Parthenon atop the Acropolis. One disparity was that Athena's temple was in a constant state of decay from the acidic pollution that was taking its toll. Even considering the couple of millennia between the temple and the house, I fantasized that the ongoing threat to the Parthenon would not be the fate of my family's house. It had withstood the ravages of the smoke and soot belched from area mills when they operated at full blast. If it could survive those, I surmised it could withstand the ravages of time.

With my arms folded, I leaned against my Mustang, which I'd parked across the road from the house, and studied the structure. The house sported the same light-brown aluminum siding accentuated by dandelion-yellow awnings my mother had put on in the 1950s. To some, the colors might now look boring and dull by twenty-first century standards, yet when contrasted with the house's original white paint framed by the coal-black trim, it blazed in technicolor. Of course, only those who saw the house back in its prime could appreciate the contrast. I mused about life there, the distant past quite alive in my memory. The reel flashed in nanoseconds from boyhood to young adulthood, with a mix of people, events, and settings. What a ride, I thought. So much of who I am is rooted there.

I glanced up and down the street and took in the kaleidoscope of architecture that prevailed. No two houses looked alike. In fact, each was unique, not only in colors but also style. In that regard, the neighborhood was vibrant with diversity even though back in my day, it was decidedly white ethnically, working class economically, and Catholic or mainstream Protestant religiously. It was a rich environment to have grown up in.

I walked down the road a bit to get a better view of the hillside that formed the house's backyard. I was dismayed to see that from where the chicken coop once stood and continuing up the hillside, it had been allowed to return to its feral state. It was a wild thicket of trees and tangled briars likely identical to the foliage my father had cleared away many decades ago and which we, his children, held at bay after his death. I shook my head as I squinted in sadness and shrugged. Well, I thought, one day Ma Nature might reclaim all this.

A voice disturbed my reverie. "Can I help you?"

I looked over to a man standing in the front yard behind an overgrown hedge. I shook my head. "No. Sorry for bothering you. I used to live in your house. Just taking a stroll along memory lane."

"Ah. I was afraid you might be casing the place. We've had a couple of burglaries in the neighborhood lately."

"Wow. Sorry to hear that. It's hard to believe. When I was a boy, that thought never crossed our minds. People often left their homes unlocked when they left for a short time."

"The good ol' days, eh?"

I crossed the road and edged closer as I talked. "They were in countless ways. We didn't have much and times were often tough, but we had gold with everything else. Forgive me for being forward, but would you mind if I check out the upper part of your yard? We used to cultivate an amazing garden up there: corn, tomatoes, cucumbers, peppers, beets. It helped keep us fed through the winter."

"Sure. You're welcome to go up, but it might be tough to get through. It's really overgrown."

"When we were kids, those woods were our playground. If we couldn't get through, we'd use a sickle to whack the weeds and clear a path."

"Those were the days. My kids wouldn't be caught dead up there. To them, it's scary. They'd rather play video games or shoot hoops on a playground."

"They'll never know what they're missing."

"Nope. I need to get back in, but you're welcome to come on up."

"Thanks. I'm thinking of accessing it from the cemetery. There used to be a path between them."

"I doubt if there's one now." The man pointed to the cargo shorts I was wearing. "You might consider slipping on some jeans. Those thickets can get pretty gnarly."

I smiled. "I'll be fine. My body has aged since I played in those woods, but the spirit of that boy remains alive and well."

I turned to leave, then turned again and waved before making my way back to my car. It was a typical Western Pennsylvania overcast day. A veneer of clouds formed a gray sky and forced the sun to work extra hard to shine through. Even though it was fall, the air was still and sultry, though not heavy with the sticky humidity common there during the dog days of August. Over the decades since I'd left, I'd become acclimated to the thin, dry air of the Colorado high country. Like the ponderosa pines and spruce trees of home sucking in the moisture of a rainfall after a dry spell, I soaked in the moisture but remained grateful that it would be only for a short stretch. As I climbed back into my Mustang, I smiled thinking of the damp, sometimes soaked with sweat, sheets I slept on as a kid while resisting the effort to climb out of my skin. Waves of cool, dry air cascaded over my body when I turned up the blower.

I put the car in neutral and allowed it to coast slowly down the road, but at the Big Hill, I kept my foot lightly tapping the brake. As I drifted, I recalled how on summer days I'd race friends on bikes, not only down the hill but also back up it, a race I invariably won. I had a distinct advantage. Actually, two. I didn't have one of those fancy American bikes weighted down with thick fenders, a chrome passenger seat, and a handlebar with grips, streamers, and a bell. Instead, I rode a bare-bones German model. Plus, it was powered by strong leg muscles that grew stronger day by day by running up and over the hills.

I negotiated the ninety-degree curve at the bottom of the hill, put the car in gear, and then slowly drove to the bridge where we'd wait for the old brown school bus to chug up the hill belching smoke and making a horrible noise when the driver shifted gears. I sat for a moment at the stop sign and recalled the fall days when my sisters, friends, and I stood there, the air heavy with dew and scented with decaying leaves. The scene was eternal and unchanging in my memory.

I made a right onto the main road and then veered onto Township Road. As I drove up it, I wondered if making the hard right from Township onto Wilmerding Road would be easier than it used to be. The turn was an acute thirty-degree angle onto an uphill trajectory. To avoid drifting backward, stalling the engine, or burning the clutch when pulling out, I had to master working the clutch efficiently when learning to drive. It took time to perfect the art, and when I did, I couldn't have been prouder. This time, to my delight, I did it with ease. I hadn't lost the touch.

Still, the blind curve made me wonder why there wasn't more carnage on those hilly, winding, often narrow Western Pennsylvania roads. It was a testament to the people, I concluded. They might speak in a colloquial form of English with words and phrases undecipherable to those not from the burgh, but they were strong, ever alert, adaptable risk-takers. I came from a hardy stock.

Nearing the entrance to the cemetery, I flipped on my turn signal, downshifted, and slowed. A loud, prolonged honk startled me, and I glanced into the rearview mirror to see a car so close, I couldn't see its front. The driver's left arm was raised out his window with his middle finger rigidly pointed upward.

"Good lord," I said aloud. "I have my signal on." As he tore by, the guy gave me an extra gesticulation and loud honk. I shook my head and quickly glanced skyward. "Thanks, Dad. You saved me again."

As I drove slowly around the cemetery's loop road, I noted that the road was gravel. In times past, I recalled it being paved with chip and seal. I noticed too that the pagoda, which was always a point of interest, was not there. In its place was nothing, just a vacated space, probably waiting to be occupied by dead bodies. Otherwise, it seemed at first glance to be much the same as when I last saw it decades ago. But then I noticed something different. The trees that were spaced throughout the cemetery were smaller and less mature. I wondered if the original trees had died or become overgrown and new ones had recently been planted to take their places.

After parking, I started to head toward the slope that led down to my old backyard, but I was distracted by something else that felt odd: warmth from the sunshine. Gazing up, I saw that the clouds had given way to blue sky. A few white, fluffy cumulus clouds floated overhead. It felt good. Embracing but a bit strange. Ten minutes earlier, it had been heavily overcast and sultry. Even in Colorado, which is famous for quick weather changes, that rapid shift in conditions would seem extraordinary. Giving it no further thought, I shrugged my shoulders. "I'll take it," I said to no one.

I recalled the exact point where the path had been and was prepared to bushwhack my way through the weeds, trees, and brambles but was surprised to see that I didn't need to find it. The path was not only there, it looked well-worn.

I was surprised. It was curious given what the current owner of my family's home had said. I sauntered down the path and quickly came to an open area of green grass. Georges' yard, I thought. The Georges had lived two doors up from us. I recalled Mr. George as a quiet, unassuming man who took great pride in his yard. He didn't plant a vegetable garden like we did, but he cultivated an array of perennials, leafy deciduous trees, and a variety of shrubs and bushes. He was meticulous about keeping the shrubs trimmed and the grass mowed. It was pleasing to see how the current owners carried on his tradition.

I continued down the path through a wooded, thick area. Masters' yard. The Masters lived next door. Mr. Masters, like our neighbor on our other side, wasn't as dedicated as Mr. George about clearing and maintaining the upper portion of his lot. But that was okay by us because it gave our yard a secluded open space boxed in on three sides by trees where we could hang out. A sense of nervous anticipation began to set in. A few steps farther and I would be in what was once my family's yard. I braced myself, but I wasn't prepared for what I saw when I stepped from the trees. In front of me lay a well-tended garden with rows of corn, tomato plants properly staked, cucumber and squash vines abundantly spreading, lush pepper plants, and green and red beet leaves that stood nearly a foot high. I held my breath. It couldn't be possible, yet there it was.

"Oh my God," I whispered as I scanned the scene. "All I need to see now is a large white rabbit hopping by and checking his wristwatch."

I stepped furtively into the garden and saw a man in brown trousers and a white tank undershirt hoeing the corn rows. He was of medium height with a receding hairline and thinning brown hair, and he was solidly built with strong muscles and chest. He appeared to be in his mid to late thirties and looked strangely familiar. But that couldn't be. None of this could be real. I stepped farther into the garden, from where I could see the area beyond it that led down to the house. It too was cleared and neatly mowed. A push mower with a yellow wooden handle sat underneath one of the cherry trees. *This is crazy. I just saw this from the road below, and it was wildly overgrown.*

The man stopped hoeing, looked up, and smiled. He pulled a handkerchief from his pocket, wiped his brow, and leaned on the hoe. His eyes were a rich brown, framed by full eyebrows. His face shone with sweat, and his broad smile revealed immaculate white teeth. It was all too strange, yet I didn't feel threatened. In fact, I felt strangely at peace. Wonder filled me.

"Welcome," he said. "Out for a walk through the woods?"

"Ah, no," I replied tentatively. "I guess I'm a bit confused. I wasn't expecting to see a garden here. I assumed it would be wooded and thick with brush."

The man smiled and shrugged. "I guess you were wrong. I've been tending this garden for quite some time."

"And no one knows it's here besides you?"

"Well, there are those who do, but they let it be. It's become my little sanctuary. When I need to escape, this allows me space and quiet time for reflecting."

The man leaned the hoe against a tree and sat down on a nearby stump. Next to it was a dinged up metal bucket with a ladle sticking out of it. He lifted the ladle, took a few sips from it, and turned the handle toward me.

"Care for a drink? I'm sorry I don't have a cup for you. I generally don't get visitors, so I wasn't expecting anyone to show up today."

"No. But thank you. I have my water bottle." I held it up to show the man.

The man eyed it curiously. "May I look at it?"

I handed him the hard plastic sports bottle.

The man turned it around in his hand, then he raised it overhead and squinted through the translucent orange plastic. "Interesting." He tapped it with his knuckles. "Pretty hard. Not breakable? It looks like there's a straw of some sort in it. How does it work?"

I took the bottle and tilted the top toward the man. "You see this nipple? When you want to drink, you bite down lightly with your teeth and then suck the water out like this." I took a sip.

"May I try?"

I looked warily at him but handed him the bottle. He did as I directed, smiled, and handed it back to me. "I like that. Much better than the canteens we had in the Army. They were round and covered with canvas. You had to screw the lid off to get a drink."

That piqued my curiosity because I recalled seeing canteens like that in Army surplus stores when I was a kid, and the man didn't seem to be very old. In fact, he looked considerably younger than me. I sat down on the grass in front of him, crossed my legs, and gazed up at him.

"Army?" I asked. "When were you in the Army?"

"Oh, it was a few years back." He took another drink from the ladle and wiped his mouth dry by brushing it against his forearm. "What brings you here?"

"Honestly, I don't know. You might call me a spiritual nomad traversing the land in search of answers."

"Answers to what?"

I sucked in my upper lip and stared off in the direction of the trees that bordered the garden. "That's the crazy part. I don't know." I turned back to the man. "It's funny. I kept trying to delineate questions on my drive across the country to here. I came up with a few, but now they seem trivial, meaningless. In fact, none of them come to mind now."

"Where's home?"

"Colorado, in the Rocky Mountains."

The man crossed his arms and stretched his legs. He said nothing, as if waiting for me to continue.

"I've lived a long life," I added, "and I've learned much. But it seems I haven't learned a scintilla of what's important or meaningful. Like why? Why life? Why anything? What's important?"

"You've thrown a new word at me. I think you said *scintilla*."

"Yes, sorry. Scintilla is a trace, a tiny bit. It comes from the same Latin word as science."

"Ah, yes. I knew that once. It's been quite some time since I heard it being used."

He nodded in understanding as he looked at me, and I began to feel self-conscious under his gaze, as if I were being studied. I felt my face flushing, and I wanted to break the silence but couldn't think of what to say.

"I don't want to sound pretentious," I finally blurted out with my voice slightly tinged with discomfort. "I guess I'm kind of flustered. Maybe I should just shut up."

The man's smile immediately put me at ease.

"No, you shouldn't. You've obviously learned much, and it's important that you talk about it and keep asking questions in the process. It's the only way to help others like me become smarter, better."

I squinted with my left eye and cocked my right one. "If you don't mind me asking, and please tell me it's none of my business if you would rather not tell me, what's your level of education? Something tells me you're far wiser and more learned than you let on."

The man shifted a bit and sat more erect. "I don't mind answering your question. But I want to be sure

I answer it accurately. You see, like you, I'm still learning and have a way to go. Right now, I'm taking a time-out to decide what my next step will be."

I sat quietly, taking in what the man said, trying to digest and fathom the obscurity of it. He had both answered and not answered my question. That made me even more curious. He seemed an unaffected, simple man who was comfortable in his own skin. Yet he projected an intelligent, wise demeanor, which belied his ordinary, unpretentious dress and manner. I studied his apparel more closely. The man was wearing tan pleated trousers and scuffed, broken leather shoes of a style long past. Behind him, a white cotton short-sleeve shirt hung on a branch. He wore no cap and was richly tanned. He came across as healthy, physically and mentally, and comfortable with who and where he was, like some brilliant professor who lectured at Johns Hopkins but found comfort and escape in the ordinary—like a garden.

Despite my advanced degree and years of study afterward, I concluded I was in over my head and was being schooled by one superior and beyond my plane of experience. I've stumbled into Epicurus's garden, and Plato is the guest lecturer, I mused. I searched my mind, trying to find the right question but couldn't find it, so I closed my eyes and took a deep breath. Just be honest, I thought. He's inside my head, and he knows it. I noticed my throat tightening and my breath becoming shallow and short. I spoke haltingly.

"I don't know what to say, where to begin. I feel like I've entered another dimension. When I first saw this garden, I jokingly thought I might see the white rabbit from *Alice in Wonderland* hopping by and checking his wristwatch. But I'm not so sure. I mean, this is real. Yet it seems surreal."

"*Alice in Wonderland* wasn't something we were taught in school. But I remember my daughters talking excitedly about it when they were in grade school." He smiled mischievously and stood. "Maybe you'll see a white rabbit. After all, this is a garden and there is plenty for one to nibble on."

He reached down, grabbed me by my wrist, and pulled me to my feet without much effort. "Let's walk a bit. I'll show you a few things that might help clear up some of your confusion."

We walked through a grove of apple and cherry trees to the top of the hill above the house I grew up in. When I saw the house, I was dumbfounded. It looked vastly different from how it looked when I viewed it from the road. It was the original white with black trim. And the dormer my mother had added by raising the rear roof was not there. It looked just like it had when it was built, just before America entered the Second World War. Immediately below us sat a chicken coop with hens and a rooster pecking the ground behind a chicken wire enclosure. Fruit trees dotted the lush green hillside, which was evenly mowed, with an extensive row of grapevines hanging with bunches of purple and green grapes separating the lower yard from the upper yard on one side of the hill.

I gasped and stood agape as my eyes misted. "I'm back in time."

I turned to the man, who gently smiled, and shook my head as tears rolled down my cheeks. "Dad?" I whispered.

He nodded. "Yes. What you're thinking is true. I am your father, and you are my son." Pointing at a rough-hewn log that he had made a bench out of, he said, "Let's sit there. You probably need a few moments to collect yourself. It was that way with me."

I sat down next to him. "With you? You've gone through something similar?"

"Remember, you and I had a similar life experience. We both lost our fathers at a very early age. You weren't quite four years old when I left, and I was only five when my father left."

"Did you see him like this?"

"Not the same situation, but yes. For the most part, you and I have different interests. I loved to golf, hunt, and tinker. From what I could observe, none of those interest you."

"Uh, no."

"You seem to like books and stories and have a strong interest in mystical stuff. Yours is a world of ideas. Mine was more, shall I say, practical."

"Well, you were a Capricorn, and I'm an Aquarius."

My father looked at me quizzingly. "As I said, mystical."

I smiled in acknowledgment.

"I sense, though, that the one interest or pastime we share is gardening."

"From the time I was a boy, I've loved playing in the mud, as I call it. It started right here when we'd play in our little camp. Then when I got older, I'd help Mum plant and take care of the garden. It's kind of paradoxical, being an air sign, but it goes to show how complex people are. Full of contradictions. But, oh boy. You're creating more questions for me."

He smiled. "I'll do my best to answer what I can. Knowing you, you'll probably ask some I can't answer, mainly because I haven't learned the answers yet."

I nodded and looked down the hill I'd played on and mowed. I tried to organize my thoughts but quickly concluded the conversation would go where it would and turned back toward my dad.

"You said you had a similar experience seeing your father, my grandfather. I never met him, of course, and sad to say, very little was spoken about him when I was growing up."

"Like you, when I grew older, I wanted to learn more about him because I also didn't know much about him. All I knew was that he migrated from

Croatia and was killed on the job in a factory. That only told me how he died, not how he lived. My mother, your grandmother, didn't wanted to talk about him or how he died when I was growing up. She seemed to want to put that painful experience behind her. So we went on with life. That was the way it was. But unlike your mother, my mother remarried, and I, along with my brothers and sisters, became part of that family.

"But my last name was different from my step-brothers and stepsisters, and that made me feel different. When I was in my teens, I learned from the men in town who had known my father that he was a craftsman and used one of their sheds as a workshop. So I went looking for it."

"You found it?"

"I did. The shed still stood. His workbench and the hooks on which he hung his tools were there, but the shed was empty. Many years later, I got to wondering if the shed was still standing. It was, but when I got nearer, I saw that it had been fixed up, and I could hear someone inside. I knocked on the door, and a man said to come in. When I went in, he turned, smiled, and said he was expecting me. I was as confused as you were when you saw me. It took me a lot longer to come to accept and understand that it wasn't some apparition but that he was truly my father, your *deda*." He turned, looked at me, and set his hand on my knee. "You see, that's another difference between us. You are far more open and sensing than I was. I was very rigid in my thinking."

"Thank you for telling me that. There's so much I'd love to know about him. Did you ask him about his life, where he grew up in Croatia, and about his coming to America? What it was like for him trying to make a new life under brutal conditions?"

"I did, and he told me about wanting to start a new life in America because of how difficult it had become in Croatia at that time. And he talked a bit about meeting my mother after arriving here and how hard and dangerous life was then."

"Did you learn anything that surprised you?"

"We talked, much as you and I are, about what is ultimately important. Like I said, I didn't think and look at life the way you do. When I was little, I could only imagine what he was like. I thought I wanted to be just like him, but as I grew, I came to understand that I couldn't be and shouldn't try to be. When we talked, I learned that in some ways, we were alike, but in most others, we were very different. Like you and me, he and I shared one common interest. We both loved tinkering, working with our hands, so that was why we met in his workshop—just like you and me meeting in this garden. You see, son, no matter their differences, there's always a place where a father and son can meet."

His last words reverberated within me. I was struck by his simple yet profound insight.

"Dad, you've just said something I'm afraid is lost on so many men. It disturbs me when I witness or hear about fathers who reject their sons outright or at least keep them at arm's length because they don't follow their father's prescribed way of life. Things like their sexual orientation, lifestyle, career choice, or following a different religious or spiritual path. I feared that might have been true about you had you lived, so I'm relieved to hear you say there's always a place where a father and son can meet."

"Well, son, you might be giving me too much credit. If I had lived to see you grow into the man you've become, I might well have been like those fathers and not handled it well. Apparently, times have changed considerably since I lived. I'd like to think that if I were alive now, I'd have a more enlightened perspective. But then, maybe not. Life has a way of causing many to lose perspective on what is most important."

"Messing with our heads is the way I'd put it. Maybe that's part of the battle each of us faces throughout our earthly existence: figuring out and focusing on what is truly important."

"I agree. Perhaps though, we should switch gears and talk about something else you're curious about."

I laughed, and he looked at me curiously. "Did I say something funny?"

"No, it was the metaphor you used to change the subject: switch gears. That's another area of common ground we share. I know how to drive a stick."

He cocked his eye. "You *are* an odd one."

We both laughed.

"Okay, on a more serious note, I'm curious about you and the countless others who die and leave this plane so young in life. It never seemed right or just to me. You at least reached middle age, but *deda* didn't even make that. He was only thirty-five. Then there are babies, children, and young adults who die either from natural causes or accidents. Why? Why do they get cheated out of living a full life? I don't get it."

"That's one of the questions I can't answer. It's not that I don't want to, but like I said, it's because I'm still learning. As you say, both my father and I died long before we grew old in Earth time. That might mean we need or want to live again so we can learn the lessons we had set out to learn or finish what we set out to accomplish. But then, maybe not. Maybe it was part of our life's lesson plan."

I sat quietly trying to ingest what my father had shared.

"You see, before returning to this plane, a soul, as you might call one's unique aspect of the Ultimate, along with, let me say, its spiritual advisors, decides what's important for its progression."

"You say 'its' not his or her."

"That's because where I am, gender is irrelevant, even though there are differences that separate each entity."

"Now you really have me thinking. What separates each entity from the others?"

He stole a sideways glance at me and smiled almost mischievously. "It would be better for you to learn more about that from one far wiser than me."

"Who?"

He winked. "You'll find out soon."

He placed his hand atop mine, turned, and sat quietly gazing out at what, in a moment in time, had been. His look portrayed a mix of longing and melancholy as if this would be the last time he would see and be part of something he had treasured.

Feeling the warmth of his touch, I turned and looked out over the expanse that appeared as it existed before my time: the house, the chicken coop my father had built, the yard with the fruit trees he planted, and the cement steps he formed and poured by hand. I was astounded anew at the skills and energy my father had during his life. His drive, his passion. Then I recalled that he'd been a Capricorn, so his focus on the land, home, and practical side of life was not surprising. These were everyday realities of human life. He had been the salt of the earth.

I, though, am quite different in my outlook. While I enjoy getting my hands in the muck through gardening and occasionally dive into home repair ventures, my mind's focus is perennially in the clouds, in the ethereal. I thrive on the unknown, the curious, sometimes obsessively so, and about what makes it all tick: Earth, the universe, life, consciousness, the collective unconscious. I ask big questions: Why do people do what they do? Why do people believe as they do? I was on a great search for meaning, purpose, and being.

I sometimes sardonically wonder if it's all merely a farce with no meaning or purpose. Are we little fools building sandcastles on the cosmic seashore and convincing ourselves that they're reality until we watch in disbelief as the tide invariably rolls in and obliterates them? Does our indomitable human spirit leave us undeterred to begin anew and build another version of the sandcastles, this time more solid and buttressed by a seawall that prevents the ocean from wiping them away, only to witness the same cosmic force leveling our puny human efforts again and again?

I was grappling with what was just revealed to me. It was beyond my comprehension, but perhaps it wasn't necessary to comprehend and completely come to know it. My job, it seemed, was to witness, marvel, and ask questions.

My father spoke as he clutched my hand tightly. "I can clarify one confusion for you. Our relationship was, of course, father and son. But that was only in that lifetime for that purpose. That was the way it had to be for you and me. Just know that is not always the case. Still, for us, for you and me at this moment in timelessness, you *still* are my son."

My eyes welled up again with tears. "I cannot tell you how long I've longed to hear those words. I'm breathless, but I suppose that doesn't matter since we're in a place where breathing might not be a fact of existence."

"That's not exactly true. All conscious beings inhale the prana, which is vital no matter a soul's level of consciousness. But again, I'll let another explain that more fully."

"Sounds good. You realize that you have my head spinning like Linda Blair's in *The Exorcist.*"

He gave me a curious look.

"Oh, sorry. That was a movie made about twenty years after you, uh, left this plane."

"You were going to say *die* weren't you."

"Yeah." I nodded sheepishly.

"It's okay. Talking about dying makes many uncomfortable. That's why people often use words or phrases like *departed* or *passing over* instead of *died.* There's probably some psychology behind that, but you'd be better at explaining it than me."

"Maybe. But I know from experience that talking about dying makes many squeamish. The most courageous people to me are those who accept their ending matter-of-factly, even serenely. I love what one man said on his deathbed: It was a privilege to be alive. That statement made me think about how we focus so much on human rights to be or do whatever, but we rarely think about the fact that we had no right to have been born in the first place."

"Interesting," he replied. "I'd never thought of it that way. But now that you said it, I like it."

"I suppose some might think I have a morbid sensibility because I often ponder not only what lies ahead after this life but what it'll be like when it comes time to depart. I'm old enough now to know it'll come soon. I just hope I handle it well and go out with dignity."

I paused and looked at him. It seemed strange to be having a conversation about death with him.

"But enough about death and dying, Dad. I'd like to talk about us, our family, but that would probably open a Pandora's box of stuff best left alone."

"Pandora's box. What's that?"

"It's a concept from Greek mythology about a woman who was too curious for her own good. She was given a most beautiful box but was told never to open it. Of course, she did and out flew every ill that humanity would have to deal with. The good news was she closed it just before hope, the remaining spirit, could escape. The notion has become a symbol in our language for getting into topics that are very painful and probably won't get resolved if talked about."

He smiled. "I see. It could get complicated. I agree, so let's not. Besides, this is about you and me."

He turned again and gazed out over the neighborhood and onto the horizon. I looked sideways at him. At first glance, he looked pensive, deep in thought. But then again, he didn't. His look was more one of wistfulness with a tinge of regret. I followed suit and took in the scene he was gazing at. It was beautiful. The fruit trees were leafy and full of ripened fruit—apples, peaches, and cherries. Bunches of purple and green grapes hung from the grapevines. The flower garden my mother had kept was ablaze with irises, marigolds, and daisies, and I inhaled their sweet aroma. I could feel the slight breeze and the sun's warmth. Yet something was missing. Every sensory perception was active except for one. Sound.

I could hear my father's voice and the rustling of leaves, but that was it. It dawned on me that I hadn't been hearing any extraneous sounds from human activity, the white noise and humdrum of daily life: traffic noise, children playing, neighbors' voices. My father and I were the only humans there. And when I listened more closely, I realized there was no sound of bird chirps. I looked over to where the chickens had been strutting and pecking and saw that they were no longer there, even though the coop and chicken wire enclosure were. The place seemed to be slowly fading away.

I reflected on what was unfolding before me, working to set incredulity aside. Whatever it was, it was real. I wasn't hallucinating or dreaming. This wasn't a mirage or vision playing out in my imagination. The entity I was sitting next to and talking with was real. I had physically touched him and felt the warmth of his skin. He was wearing real clothes and doing real stuff. I furrowed my brow in confusion and slowly shook my head. Was I directing the events of a lucid dream and slowly awakening? "Am I in a dream state and just imagining this?" I spluttered.

"No, son. You're not dreaming or imagining this. This is real, but on this plane, reality is unlike what you have experienced up to now."

He stretched and waved his arm across what lay before us. "All this is real because it once existed. Once something exists or happens, it endures forever. Every action, every event, every word spoken or thought can never be erased. In this case, this is exactly as I once saw it. It has been etched into my cosmic memory. And you have entered my space."

"So one can go back in time?"

"Yes, but why go back if there's no reason to? At times, there *is* a reason, like for me, right now."

My eyes widened. "I think I know the answer to this, but maybe not. What's your reason?"

"There are two, in fact. The first is for me to meet with you and have this talk. One regret I had when I passed from the life in which I was your father was that I would not see my children grow. I would not be there to help them, guide them through their years. I would not see how they turned out as adults and see what kind of lives they led and if they would have children who would be my grandchildren. Would they forget or not know me because they were too young to have vivid memories of our time together—like you?"

"I have vague memories of you, like when I'd stand on the hump on the floor of the backseat when we'd go for a ride in your Hudson and of digging through a pile of sawdust for little sacks filled with coins at your gun club picnic."

A pensive look crossed his face. "When I was dying, I felt helpless because I thought I was abandoning my family, but there was nothing I could do. And that was my final lesson. I no longer had what got me through much of my life: power and control. Then I was overcome with regret when I realized I wouldn't be there to watch my children grow. But I've learned it's necessary for everyone to live their lives and learn their life lessons no matter the circumstances. And for you that meant growing up fatherless and figuring it out on your own."

I was awed by the profundity of what my father said. The last thoughts of a dying man. There was much to unpack from his words, but I quickly decided it would be better to do that at another time. I picked up on his last point.

"Well, Dad, that I have, and to say the least, it has been a most interesting life. I rejected the prescriptive way of life, deciding that the unknown path would be my fate. Does that make sense?"

"It does. From the time of your birth, I sensed you wouldn't be like your brothers. I had a feeling but couldn't put my finger on it. Now I can. I like the way you've turned out. I'm sure you made your share of mistakes along the way, just like I did, but you seem to be happy and have lived a fulfilled life."

"True on both counts, but it's not over yet and there's more I want to explore and try to understand. So much to learn and so little time to learn it."

Sensing there was nothing either of us could add to that topic, I shifted the conversation back to him.

"You said you had two reasons for coming back. What was the second one?"

"To see this one last time, to putter in the garden. I still have attachments to it and to this place. It's one of the remaining threads connecting me to my past life. It's time for it to be cut, and as you can see, it's fading away."

I grimaced. "I get it. I dread leaving my mountains. I know full well at some point I will. But knowing something isn't like feeling it." I cleared my throat. "Dad, I hope I'm not coming across as arrogant or superior when I say this, but I assume you're not familiar with the writings of Albert Camus, the French Algerian philosopher."

"No, I'm not. I never read or got any background in philosophy, but honestly, it wouldn't have been a subject I would've had any interest in then."

"In *The Myth of Sisyphus,* he correlates longings like ours to the Greek myth of the man condemned by the gods to push a massive boulder up a hill only to see it tumble back to the bottom, where he must begin anew. His name was Sisyphus. Camus said that Sisyphus's rock is symbolic of our attachments to our earthly experiences and special places. We know that our life and everything connected to it must end, yet we desperately cling to life and life's trappings, even in the face of imminent death. From what I'm gathering, it seems that longing doesn't necessarily end as soon as we pass over."

My father sat quietly for a moment. Then he turned and faced me. "For some, like me, that attachment carries over, but not for all. I've learned that those who had pretty bad life experiences don't carry attachment or longing for the place they just left. And others who might have had a good and beautiful life-time in a place they loved often accept that it was good but also understand that it is necessary to detach from it and move on. Your mother was like that.

"She lived a hard life and endured many trials and difficulties. But she handled all the adversity with strength and nobility. She never wavered or weakened. I saw that in her character when we first met. I knew right away that she was my superior in many ways, and she was the one I was to create and raise a family with." He looked off again into the distance. "But she didn't hang around here for long after she passed over," he added with a note of sadness in his voice.

"She was pretty religious," I said. "She held fast to her Catholic faith and drilled it into us kids. But as she aged, she seemed to drift away from it. Still, she never lost her sense of the spiritual realm. From what I under-stand, though, you were quite her opposite. You didn't care much for church or religion."

"No, I didn't, but going to church or believing in a certain religion doesn't mean a person is spiritual. In my own way, I was spiritual, even though I gave little thought to an afterlife."

"That's understandable on multiple levels, Dad, given how you were shaped by societal norms about roles of men and women and how you stayed focused on the very practical aspect of supporting your large and growing family. But I get your point. So many confuse or overlap being religious with being spiritual and believe that being spiritual means praying or meditating or performing some sort of rituals. I reject that. For me, spirituality can mean just being kind to others and leading not a perfect but a good life."

"That seems very reasonable," he said after a moment. "I wish I'd thought of that when I was alive."

"You didn't need to think about it. You just did it."

I took a sip from my water bottle and offered it to him. He took it and took a long draw. When done, he tapped his knuckles again on the hard plastic.

"I like this. What will they come up with next?"

"Don't ask," I replied as I rolled my eyes. "Yes, we keep making life easier and more convenient, but all those so-called advancements come with a cost. Earth is paying the price. But that's a topic for another time if we will have another time to chat."

"You never know."

"I hope so. Dad, there was so much I wanted to ask you if I ever had the chance to talk to you, not ever thinking I might. But now that I am, and after everything I'm seeing, I'm not sure if what I thought I'd want to talk about is important. That life is past. What I am curious about is this plane you're on." I chuckled. "I was ready to say that I can't wait to get here to learn more about it, but I can wait."

He nudged me in the ribs with his elbow. "Be careful what you wish for."

He stood and pointed back toward the garden. "Even though there is no time here, it's time to go."

Once again, he grabbed me by the wrist and pulled me to my feet. We began to hike back to the garden.

"I understand," I said, "but I have to ask you about Mum. You said that she's no longer here with you. Does that mean she's advanced to a higher plane and will never return to human form?"

His eyes lit up. "She was here only briefly and has moved on to a higher level. As you said, she was the spiritual one in our marriage. As for her possibly returning here, that would be up to her, from what I understand."

"What I wouldn't give to hear her voice and see her face one more time. But I'm eternally grateful for having her as my mother. It was a privilege to be her son. And yours."

When we got to the garden, we stood quietly taking it in. He wrapped his arm around my shoulder and pulled me close.

I leaned into him. "Well, Dad, you've already answered so much, but I have to tell you that this experience has raised far more questions in my mind than it has answered."

"That's my boy. It's how you're very different from your brothers. It's the way you think. You're insatiably curious. I saw that in you as a toddler. Always getting into mischief."

"Yeah, well, I sometimes picture a whirlwind when I'm confronted with having more questions raised in the process of getting some answered. My head gets to swirling."

"That's understandable, and it's likely it will spin even more if you try to grasp all this with your human mind. But I'm not the one to answer those questions for you. There are others who will be able to answer some, if not many of them. One of them you have already encountered."

I was taken aback. "Who?"

"The same one who guided you here in the first place."

He pointed toward the stump where a woman wearing a cowboy hat and a long denim skirt sat.

My eyes widened in disbelief.

"Ann?"

Ann smiled. "Small universe, isn't it?"

PART 3

ON WINGS AND PAWS

LIKE THE PREVIOUS time I climbed up to Pueblo Alto, the air smelled fresh and clean, although this time, there was nary a whisper of a cloud. The sky was a rich blue. The previous day's gully washing downpour in Chaco Culture National Historic Park cleansed the air of microscopic dust particles. The storm had swept in without notice, but just as quickly, it moved out. By the morning's first light, the sky had cleared.

Gazing out over the expanse across the canyon toward Tsin Kletzin as I perched cross-legged on the remains of the Pueblo Alto wall, I felt the stillness that blanketed the canyon. It was a blessing.

Breathing the prana abounding around me, I closed my eyes and thought of the conversation I had with my dad. The fact that I'd conversed with him still boggled my mind, albeit less so now. I was coming to accept the normality of mind-boggling revelations, and I was beginning to understand that what befuddled the human mind was ordinary fare in the other dimension.

I reflected on how our talk was revelatory on two levels—the personal and the esoteric—and how both areas touched on a range of topics. The revelations from my father about my grandfather made me more curious about him and his life. I already knew my grandfather had died horrifically on his job when a beam crushed his skull. But, as my dad said, that only told how he died, not how he lived. I needed to research and learn more. What particularly intrigued me, though, was my dad sharing that he had encountered his dad much as I had him. I hadn't inherited my father's skills or interests or preferred his way of life, but that experience was a bond that only he and I shared. That made me feel more than good.

Strangely, but perhaps not so strangely, I found what he told me of the other plane intriguing, though not as meaningful as what I learned of his life. That suggested something about what was important to me. I wasn't sure what that was, but I felt comfortable knowing that in time it would be made known to me. I smiled inwardly. Perhaps I would come to that understanding once again through Ann's guiding hand.

I opened my eyes, resumed a casual sitting posture, and began nibbling on a banana I had pulled from my daypack. I was feeling a bit antsy anticipating meeting Ann here. It was her suggestion, one I took as more of a directive when we were leaving my father's garden. Periodically, I scanned the trail heading up to Pueblo Alto with the hope I'd see her hiking up. But I saw no signs of her or of any other day hiker. Perhaps, I thought, she's a late sleeper. But then, come to think about it, I didn't recall seeing her camper in the campground. Maybe she had vehicle problems or got detained for some reason. It was puzzling.

As was the phenomenon of shape-shifting. I had read about the ability of certain beings to change their appearances or forms, though I had always thought of it in more mythical ways, part of certain cultures stories. But I had experienced it with my own eyes. Coyote Man must've been a shape-shifter. While I didn't literally witness him changing into human form from coyote to man and then back, there could be no other explanation. I knew whenever I heard or saw a coyote, I'd wonder if it was him playing a trick with me.

Staring off toward the southern horizon, I noticed a bird soaring high and making huge arcing sweeps across the sky. I shaded my eyes with my hand to get a clearer picture. At first, I thought it might have been a hawk. But as it circled and gracefully banked lower and lower, I could see it was a much larger bird, maybe an eagle or an osprey. As it got closer in its descent, I could see it was neither. It had a long neck, an extended pointed beak, and long, thin legs that looked like sticks trailing behind it. As it gracefully arced and swooped overhead, I got a good view of its plumage. On the bird's back, the feathers were off-white, but on its wide wings, they were a rich grayish-blue. I had never seen such a bird in nature, but I was sure I'd seen pictures of them. I wracked my brain trying to recall the species as I watched it alight in the center of a kiva.

Stunned not only by its presence but also by its beauty, I sat in awe. It was definitely not a desert bird. It looked more like a waterfowl. I wondered if it had gotten blown off course by the previous night's storm, like the red ibis had in "The Scarlet Ibis."

"I know I'm mixing my metaphors," it said, "but I'm sure you're thinking I'm a fish out of water. But come on. You think too literally."

I beamed as I trotted down to the kiva. "Ann, you wily bird. When you said you'd meet me up here, I figured I'd see you traipsing up the trail in hiking boots with a daypack strapped to your back."

"Well, no on that. I'm afraid I don't pack that apparel. Besides, there's much more to see when flying."

Ann flapped her wings and transformed herself into human form. She was wearing the same skirt, blouse, hat, and boots she'd worn when we first met in the interior room of Pueblo Bonito. "I have to say that even though you fashion yourself to be like Jonathan in *Jonathan Livingston Seagull,* I wonder if your left brain dominates your psyche at times."

"I admit it. I'm embarrassed. Maybe it's mental muscle memory."

"That it is. Your culture is so disciplined to think in literal terms that it makes escaping its gravitational pull a superhuman feat."

"I hear you on that. It started early with my childhood Catholic education. It's taken me years to get this far. But at least I've gotten to this point."

"You have. You've grown and come far. But reconsider about whether your parochial education hindered you or whether it provided the basis for you to be where you are."

"Will do. I'll play my own devil's advocate," I said chuckling.

Ann settled into a comfortable seated posture, folding her skirt as she wrapped her legs under her. I set my daypack across from her near the edge of the kiva and leaned against it, squatting.

"I was just thinking about the conversation I had with my dad. While it gave me more information about him and other stuff, it also raised more questions for me."

"No doubt, and you might have some that even I cannot answer. Understand that there is much that is not only beyond human comprehension but also off-limits to it. It's part of the process. It's the reason why the human mind is wiped clean of prior knowledge of life beyond the human plane at birth. I believe the term psychologists use for that is tabula rasa."

"So what you're saying is that it's okay for me to be super curious and inquisitive, but it's also okay to not have my questions answered as long as I walk on Earth."

"Yes, to a degree. By your pursuit, you will come to know far more than, let's say, your average human."

"Especially the disinterested ones, I presume."

"Definitely more than the disinterested ones. But be comforted by knowing that you have plenty of company in your pursuit. Hundreds of millions are seeking just as you are. Some are open about it, but many are not."

"Why not?"

"Mostly for fear they might be considered odd, weird, or even a heretic or an embarrassment to their family."

"Well, my dear Ann, I crossed that bridge long ago."

"I know. I've been watching you."

"My guardian angel?"

"Not exactly. I wasn't guarding or protecting you. I was that little voice that kept pushing you, prodding you, especially in your young adulthood, to travel from your safe places, talk to others who held different points of view, and try to comprehend why they held their viewpoints. The goal was to open your mind, which was fairly closed."

I screwed up my face. "Ouch. That wasn't pleasant to hear, but I know you're right. The crazy part was that I hated that, and it irked me. But I can't understand why I became that way."

"You had become a doctrinaire, in large part due to taking your education too literally and dogmatically. And that conflicted with your essential nature. It was important for your development to understand that it's one thing to maintain a belief system and have opinions but quite another to be able to defend your positions rationally with evidence or explain in even tones why you have an intuitive sense about what you hold or believe."

"I did come to that understanding, but it got me into hot water with someone I'd rather not talk about."

"No need to. I observed that. I watched you spiral down, but I was confident it wouldn't break you or do you in. Over the decades prior to that, you had grown stronger and become more confident in yourself. Nevertheless, it was an ordeal you needed to endure because only by facing it head on and not allowing it to crush you could you come out stronger and more courageous. You needed to slay your fears."

"Like St. George slaying the dragon?"

Ann shrugged. "Pick your myth. It's a story that's been told and reenacted since humans awakened to and became conscious of their place among sentient life. In your case, you still had some, let me say, coarsening to do before you could pursue your late life profession as a writer and do it with a firmness of conviction. I believe you call it developing a thick skin."

Ann's reference to my having become a writer made me flash back to when my friend Daniel encouraged me to become one. It was a bittersweet memory though. Daniel's suggestion opened up a new pathway and ignited a passion within me, but it also came right before he told me he was ending our relationship. I swallowed the lump in my throat as I recalled our chat and took a deep breath before continuing.

"Well, it's not as thick as an alligator's, but I *am* better able to withstand the slings of critics' arrows." I paused a moment, considering what she'd said. "You said that what I will call my intransigence or rigidity in thought was due in large part to overdoing my parochial education, which means it wasn't the sole cause."

"No, it wasn't. You were full of fear—fearful and perhaps even terrified that your truth would be found out. So you hunkered down, built a wall around yourself, and became defensive. Part of that defense was a good offense."

I nodded and smiled sadly. "Yeah. When I was about sixteen, 'I Am a Rock' became my personal theme song, my private ethos. But having gone through that, I learned, I hope, an invaluable life lesson. Whenever I hear someone shrieking to high heaven and condemning those like me, I cringe about how much they're hiding—hiding from and hiding behind. They remind me of the line in *Hamlet* about the lady who doth protest too much, although in my experience, it's mostly been guys rending their garments in self-righteous rage doing the protesting."

"Yes, you've come far, but now you realize that you have far to go. And you've become open to that which you would have opposed in your youthful, zealous days."

"I like to think so, but it helps hearing it from someone who would know." I winked. "Like my guardian angel."

Ann smiled. "Tell me more about what you've walked away with from your conversation with your father."

"There's so much that it's hard to know where to begin. But one notion reverberates in my mind. It's why so many, if not the overwhelming majority of people, limit themselves by buying in to everything they were spoon-fed about life after death. It's sad to see how many look at their earthly existence as ultimate reality and believe that when they die, either they cease to exist or they get magically transported to another place, either as a reward or as punishment."

"I understand, but the question about what happens to the human spirit or soul after death is part of everyone's earthly experience. Considering different potentials can be hard work and seem daunting when dealing with everything else in daily life. And the notion of impermanence can be overwhelming, disconcerting, and even frightening. So many take refuge and find comfort in their beliefs of an eternal permanence, which is usually the one they were acculturated to from early childhood, or in a belief that there will be a crisp conclusion to their existence."

"I guess. I suppose that if I weren't already pre-disposed to being open to new phenomena, I'd be like that too and would not have been receptive to what you offered in our brief talk in Pueblo Bonito."

We talked about how that came together, the synchronicity of it all. I described the scene when I first spotted her from the terrace walking across the Pueblo Bonito courtyard and why I initially considered it to be merely coincidental and having no particular meaning.

"I was waiting for you," Ann said.

"You knew I'd be there?"

Ann nodded. "Recall what I said about watching you when you went through that most painful time. Rest assured that I don't hover over you and watch you at every moment. Far from it. Besides, you're not my only charge. But I was there when you were at your lowest. That's the way it works. In human terms, it's like an alarm going off. When you reach deep inside yourself in times of anguish, in one way or another, it sounds the alarm. And we're there to buoy you up and encourage you to stand strong."

"Kind of like a cheerleader?"

"Well not so trivial as that, but you get the point. When one does some serious soul searching, it's very much a cry for help. Some resort to prayer and send an invocation to a deity or saint to help them. It doesn't matter how one does it. What matters is that one does reach beyond himself or herself, whether it's through prayer, meditation, or bellowing out in pain to the Universe."

"Like I did?"

She smiled. "A cry for help, no matter what form it's uttered, is still a cry for help."

I spoke about how, at that moment, what I had been chasing around in my mind crystallized in my soul. *Stuff* meant more than objects. It included all human affairs, ranging from the good and positive like love, kindness, and the material necessities of life to the bad and negative like hatred, violence, and excessive materialism. I gained insight into the principle that stuff played a most important role for every human being because it—personally and collectively—was the basis for what was ultimately important: how the individual responded to their stuff.

"It drove home for me the Buddhist concepts of impermanence and emptiness," I said. "Up to that point, they were vague and hard for me to get my head around."

"That's good. As you now see, your American culture, which in many ways has been the vanguard of Western Civilization over the past couple of centuries, has been in the forefront of the phenomena that have driven the West: industrialization, high-level technology, and intense individualism. The problem for many, which has become viral, to borrow a term from your medical and internet language, is that your culture has deified those things. They have been raised to the level of religion, which has also become corrupted."

"Well, I understand that Jesus said you could serve either God or money. Sadly, too many think they can do both. They insist they're serving their creator when in fact, they're worshipping what they define as success: money, power, and domination. And the most insane part is that greed and the six other deadly sins are now blatantly considered virtues."

"Yes, and your modern economic system, while lifting so many from poverty, has also left countless many behind and a path of destruction in its wake. Millions remain downtrodden, and your home, Earth, which I am part of, is being laid to waste." Ann sighed but then brightened up. "Yet there's hope. There's always that."

I shifted my weight, stretched my legs, and lifted the hose from my hydration pack to take a drink, looking at Ann curiously. "Don't you get thirsty when you're in human form. It's pretty dry here."

"I do, but this won't take long. Besides, there are hundreds of little pools I can swoop down to and get a drink from on my way back."

I smiled widely. "So in your corporeal essence, you're not a human but a bird."

"Well, yes and no. The bird is the creature I have chosen to be when I'm not in human form. My fellow beings choose different forms to appear in."

"You mean like Coyote Man, who I met the last time?"

She pointed toward my right. "You mean him?"

I turned and saw a coyote resting on its haunches at the top of the knoll. It stood and let out a howl, then trotted over next to Ann.

"Holy crap!" I said. "Coyote Man, I thought I'd never see you again."

He transformed himself into a human and, like Ann, looked the same as he had previously.

"I guess you were wrong," he said.

"I can see that, and I'm very happy I was. I was hoping we'd meet again. I have so many questions, the first being, who or what are you?"

Coyote Man spoke in a gravelly voice. "You see us as separate beings, but Ann and I are not really separate. We are both manifestations of Earth's consciousness."

He explained that when the planet took shape out of cosmic matter, it took a couple of billion years for it to stabilize sufficiently to support life. When that came about, Earth's spirit animated physical properties with aspects of consciousness inherent to it, and with that sprang life."

"What about evolution?" I asked. "Is it a fact? And if so, has the consciousness within each species, plant or animal, evolved?"

"Yes, evolution with species development is real," Coyote Man replied. "Every species evolves physically in conjunction with its unique form of consciousness. But ultimately, there is only one consciousness. Every form of consciousness, inanimate or sentient, is a part of Earth's consciousness. And Earth, like every other life-sustaining planet, is in turn an aspect of the Ultimate. It is that which you call the Universe."

"So what you're saying is that you and I, like every critter, plant, or rock, are aspects of Earth's consciousness, which is part and parcel of that Universe I trust in."

"Correct," Coyote Man said.

"Which makes me like you," I said. "But then, I'm not like you."

"You are, but not quite," Ann said. "When a spirit or soul returns to live another human life, in that lifetime, it can only be in its corporeal state of existence. Once a spirit or soul achieves what the Buddha called enlightenment, it no longer needs to return to physical form. It can if it chooses to, but it's not necessary. So the primary difference between us and you is that at this point in your evolution, you can appear only in corporeal form.

"Then there are beings like us who have taken on the role of what humans call spirit guides after attaining enlightenment. Some call us guardian angels, but that's a misnomer. We don't guard. Instead, we guide, encourage, and support."

"Fascinating. So I take it you're not avatars."

"You are correct," said Coyote Man. "Unlike us, avatars are enlightened beings who have chosen to reincarnate and live what you might call *normal* lives, although the lives they live are quite extraordinary.

"You see, it took eons for humans to evolve to a point where they could grasp deep philosophical, ethical, moral, and behavioral notions. Several thousand years ago, a few reached that level of consciousness. That's when the first avatars appeared. Some in your culture call them highly evolved souls or prophets like those in the Old Testament. But that's a matter of semantics. When the need is great, they reincarnate so they can share the wisdom they learned through their human lives. You see them as wise and noble people, but in reality, they're manifestations of the Earth spirit.

"The age of the avatars is far from over. As long as humans exist, there will be a need for great teachers to rebuke, cajole, and guide them when they go too far off course. In fact, one of the historical people you greatly admire was one."

I looked at him curiously and shrugged. "I'm at a loss."

"Think about the one you say you would love to talk to the most if you had the chance."

I beamed. "Crazy Horse. But after having the conversation I had with my dad, Crazy Horse has dropped to number two."

"Understandably," Coyote Man said. "But think about why you came to admire him so greatly."

"Well, I could go on about how he was such a great leader for his people and how he tragically suffered at the end. But I sensed there was something more to him that inspired his people. It was as if he were a messenger from *Wakan Tanka* telling them to be brave, that the Great Spirit was with them."

"That he was," said Coyote Man. "I shadowed him when he went about his mission. I knew it would end tragically, not only for him but also for his people. But it was necessary for him to do all he could to give them hope and courage in the face of brutality." He sighed as he hung his head.

Ann reached over and placed her hand atop his. She picked it up from there. "It's important to understand that certain spirit guides remain in spirit form only. Some reincarnate like the avatars you two were talking about. And there are also those like us who, when in corporeal form, appear either as human or animal depending on the need. In your language, we're called *shape-shifters*."

"I thought about that possibility," I said. "But it seems to me that while you're both shape-shifters, you're not exactly the same. Are there different kinds of shape-shifters?"

"Yes, there are," Coyote Man said. "Some are unbounded like Ann. They can be there for people no matter where they are and no matter their circumstances. Others, like me, are dedicated to a specific place that has become sacralized by the rituals performed by people, over and over. It could be a grotto, a body of water, or a church, temple, or a site like the Wailing Wall in Jerusalem. It's the reason that when you come here, you might connect with both of us. But if you went to Lourdes, you would find a local spirit to guide you."

"Yes, I recall you saying you've watched me over the years when I've hiked and done my spiritual practices. And to think that in all those times, I thought I was alone."

"Perhaps then," Ann said, "that's the greatest lesson you've—hopefully—learned: You're never alone. Loneliness is a human construct. It's understandable when people feel lonely, given your intrinsic need for human companionship. But when that feeling arises, it's important to recall that in the greater scheme of existence, you're not alone."

"Well, so much for existentialism," I quipped.

Ann and Coyote Man looked at each other. Ann rolled her eyes and Coyote Man shrugged his shoulders.

"You know, Ann, there is only so much we can do," Coyote Man said. And both burst out laughing.

"Okay, I'll be serious now," I said. "On the one hand, it makes sense, but on the other, it's still mind-blowing. With so much to get my head around, it'll take time for me to fully internalize all this."

138 | Jerry Fabyanic

"Take a minute now," Ann said, "and meditate. Allow yourself a few moments to begin processing what we've shared."

I closed my eyes, pinched my thumbs to the middle fingers, and began taking deep breaths. After doing an eight-count, I opened my eyes, and before me were Ann and Coyote Man in their animal forms.

I smiled. "At some point, I'd like to do that."

"You will soon," Ann said.

"How do you know that?" I asked.

Ann smiled wryly. "Let's just say some little bird told me."

"I'd like that. That would be heaven. But when I reach that level, I'd rather be able to reappear as something other than a bird or coyote, meaning no offense of course."

"None taken," she said. "You can choose whatever animal form is in existence at the time. But it would need to be one that shares the same terrain as humans. So not a dolphin, for example, or one that might be going extinct."

"Like polar bears?"

She nodded.

"May I ask why you chose your animal forms?"

"When I was in human form long ago, I admired birds," Ann said. "I found that I could talk to them, even the most predatory ones. If I were fully human today, I would be an ornithologist. Coming to see you this time, I thought it would be fun for me to do something extraordinary—like appear as a bird not associated with the desert. I chose to be a blue heron because of the symbolism associated with it."

"Yes, that's it! A heron. I couldn't put my finger on what kind of bird was flying around. But now I recall that. In Greek mythology, the blue heron was a messenger, like Hermes. I think it was Athena, the goddess of wisdom, and Aphrodite, the goddess of love, who would send it."

"Yes," said Ann. "And among some of the indigenous tribes of North America, the blue heron symbolizes self-determination, meaning one who chooses to follow their own path."

"I like that. How about you, Coyote Man?"

"When I began to appear among the peoples who first settled on these lands, I discovered how highly esteemed the coyote was among them. For many, the coyote was the Trickster. I liked that because tricking people doesn't need to be mean or malicious. It can be humorously lighthearted and still convey wisdom. I realized that people like to be tricked or fooled, like with magicians. It stretches their thinking skills and imaginations, and when done in the right spirit, it can make them smile and even be happy when sad, if only for a moment. And sometimes someone has to be tricked to help save them. So from then on, I have reappeared in coyote form."

"And when you appear in human form, why are you dressed like a Native American from that epoch?"

"Why not?"

"Oh, I can't think of a reason. It just seems out of place?"

"Out of place? This isn't exactly a center of modern civilization. We're in an area deemed a national park by your people to preserve the history and legacy of the people who made this their spiritual center."

"True. I just thought you'd be dressed like Ann in something more related to this time."

"You mean like you are?" He let out a howl and shook his head. "I wouldn't be caught dead in something so ordinary as that. That would be gauche."

I laughed. "Fair enough. It's good to see that spirits from the other realm have a sense of humor."

"When you do what we do," Ann said, "having a sense of humor along with a fondness for irony is requisite. Think about who our clientele is."

With that, Ann began dancing and chirping in singsong and Coyote Man lifted his head and howled.

"Okay, okay," I said after a bit. "Calm down. You've shown me there's truth to the old adage about people being proof God has a sense of humor."

I pushed myself up to a standing position, put my hands together, and bowed before Blue Heron and Coyote.

"With much gratitude," I said.

Ann fluttered her wings and bowed her long neck. Then she spread and flapped her wings and gracefully lifted off. She made several passes overhead, circling higher and higher, and then headed south.

After Ann departed, Coyote Man trotted up to me, lowered his head, and lifted a paw. I took it in my hand and shook it.

"Thank you, wise one," I said bowing in return.

Coyote Man stepped back, howled one more time, and trotted off in the direction of New Alto.

—w—

ACKNOWLEDGMENTS

MY THANKS TO family, friends, and readers, known and unknown, for encouraging me to keep moving forward with my writing. Your words give me the impetus and fortitude to expand my repertoire by intrepidly venturing into the deeper dimensions of mind and spirit and making concepts from them more easily accessible and understandable through storytelling.

A major thank you to Andrea Antico, Judith Janson, Pat Foote, Verena Andersen, Mary Lou Secor, and Laurel McHargue for critiquing and offering most helpful feedback on the drafts of *Chacolata*, as well as for endorsing it. Your insights were a reminder about how a story itself, along with particular passages, scenes, and characters in it, resonate more strongly with different readers.

A note of gratitude for my ongoing publishing triad: Melanie Mulhall, Nick Zelinger, and Veronica Yager. Thank you, Melanie, for making my words sing and dance and for being a trusted source of insight and clarity into the philosophical, psychological, and mythological realms I explore in my stories. Thank you, Nick, for your stellar work done by drawing from your reservoir of artistic talent to create eye-catching covers for my books and to lay out the text so readers can easily move through it. Thank you, Veronica, for your expertise and guidance vis-à-vis the most esoteric of realms for me: technology.

Lastly, I thank the muses and spirit guides who inspired and unconsciously shepherded me throughout the writing process.

ABOUT THE AUTHOR

JERRY FABYANIC is the award-winning author of fiction and nonfiction books. Jerry's novels are theme focused and character driven, and his essays explore a wide range of mind and spirit topics. Using metaphors, allusions, and symbolism as vehicles, Jerry probes answers to his perennial Big Question: Why do people believe and act as they do? Jerry brings what might be arcane and complex philosophical, psychological, and mythological concepts into the world of everyday understanding and meaning.

Jerry inveterately finds meaning in places, events, and synchronistic occurrences. Chaco Canyon, which is located in Chaco Culture National Historic Park, New Mexico, is one of those places." Chaco has held deep meaning for Jerry since his first visit there. As it was for the indigenous people who constructed the sites and positioned the rock slabs atop Fajada Butte (the Sun Dagger) to keep track of the cycles of both the sun and the moon beginning around 800 CE, Chaco has become Jerry's primary spiritual center. Each time he visits it, he not only feels a special reverence for the land and the structures, he also feels a connection to those ancient peoples and to his fellow spiritual travelers who also find personal connections to Chaco.

Jerry encourages you to learn more about the marvels of Chaco along with the mysteries it holds by going to Anna Sofaer's website, The Solstice Project, *https://solsticeproject.org/*. There you'll not only be able to learn about the researchers' basic archaeological findings, but you'll also have the opportunity to better understand the complex astronomical significance of the structures, their layout and positioning, and the artwork depicted in petroglyphs throughout the canyon.

Learn more about Jerry and his writings and sign up for his monthly essay at *https://jerryfabyanic.com/*.

POST-READING DISCUSSION AND JOURNALING TOPICS

Do you have a special sacred place in nature? If so, describe it and reflect on what makes it sacred for you?

Do you believe in reincarnation? If so, do you believe or have a sense that you've lived before? Describe that or those experiences as best you can.

Do you agree with Ann's point that the answer can at times provide the question? Cite examples from your life.

Consider the conversation and interaction between Jonathan and his father. What does it say about them as individuals and their relationship?

Why do you suppose Jonathan's father clung to the place of his last incarnation while his mother didn't?

Think about the place you grew up in. Does it have special meaning for you? Are you drawn back to it either physically or in memory?

Do you think spirits have emotions and other human characteristics, like humor and a sense of irony?

Do you believe gender exists in the world beyond? If so, is it relevant? Explain.

Do you agree that talking about dying makes many uncomfortable? If so, why is it the case?

Do you agree or disagree with Ann's contention that many take refuge and find comfort in their belief of an eternal permanence because of what they were taught as children or because their beliefs provide a crisp conclusion to their existence?

Do you have a spirit animal or feel a special or symbiotic relationship or connection to a certain animal? If so, name it and identify the characteristics of it that you find admirable or perhaps reflect an aspect of your psychological or emotional being.

Do you believe shape-shifters are real or are they only imaginings of myth, perhaps symbolic of human behaviors? Explain.

Identify a person from the past you would love to have a conversation with. Explain why. What does your choice say about you?

www.ingramcontent.com/pod-product-compliance
Lightning Source LLC
Chambersburg PA
CBHW031155020426
42333CB00013B/675